What people have to say about Erika Ginnis and Essential Mysteries: A User's Guide for the 21st Century Mystic

"The guidance and inspiration you'll find in Erika Ginnis' book absolutely changed my life. Through my work with Erika, I have come to realize my connection to spirit, claim my personal power by acting and thinking from my highest self (instead of from a place of depression, fear and lack) and put my vision into action to create the life I've always wanted.

"After a long illness and a series of failed relationships I had fallen into a destructive pattern of thinking and being that brought about increased struggle instead of the change I desired. Though traditional therapy had helped, it was finding a counselor and mentor who integrated spirituality and energy work with counseling that helped me finally break the chains that bound me. Working with Erika, I learned how to run positive healing energy and release the negative, disempowering stuff. I learned how to stay centered and keep my heart light and open even in the midst of challenges. I understood how my past patterns helped to manifest the struggles I experienced and how in creating a new vibration I could begin to live lighter—without judgment, without needing to control outcomes—and create something new and beautiful that actually helped other people in the process.

"Erika's work inspires people to live in the bright shining light of life. It is a method of navigating the ups and downs of being human that honors all experiences, perspectives and religions while opening the individual to their truest self and the myriad of opportunities that are available to them. Given where I came from and where I am now, I know that anything is possible. I am so grateful to Erika for her help and encouragement and thrilled that she wrote this book so that more people can benefit from her work."

—Susan DuMett of Vox Vespertinus; Operatic vocalist and writer, Seattle Washington

"I was experiencing emotional blockages that led to frequent illnesses and a fear of living my life to its fullest. The soothing, nurturing reassurance of Erika's good work filled me with joy. Now my life is richer and more full of love for my self and others than it has ever been! I've found that healing the emotions is much more efficient than treating the illnesses that arise from emotional blockages."

—Lori Campbell, Kirkland Washington

Essential Mysteries

Essential Mysteries

A User's Guide for the 21st Century Mystic

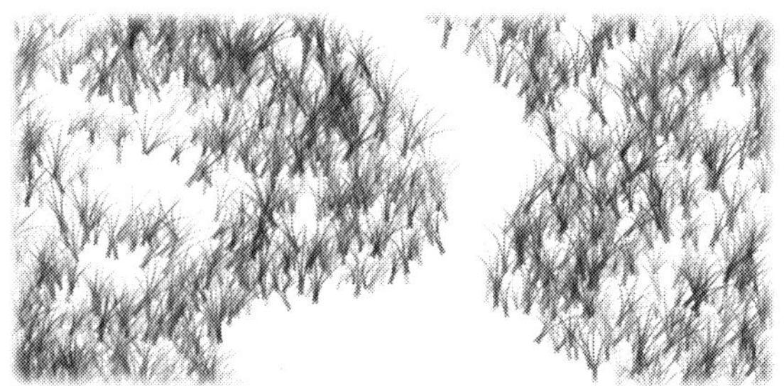

Erika Ginnis

Inbreath Communication
Pahoa, Hawaii
www.inbreathcommunication.com

ISBN 978-0-9825366-0-5
Essential Mysteries: A User's Guide for the 21st Century Mystic
1st edition, December 2009

Erika Ginnis is offering this information on training, reading, healing, and spiritual (pastoral) counseling as a certified spiritual teacher, healer, energy worker, ordained minister and pagan clergy. This work is of a spiritual nature and is not intended to take the place of treatment from a doctor or other medical professional. The author and publisher recognize the reader's autonomy, and personal responsibility in regards to using this or any other spiritual teaching, and assume no liability for actions resulting from those personal choices.

Published by Inbreath Communication
Pahoa, Hawaii USA
www.inbreathcommunication.com
Design: Inbreath Communication

Printed in the United States of America

Table of contents

Preface

This book began as a collection of essays and talks, published and unpublished, that span the years between 1984 and 2006 and is influenced by a number of spiritual traditions. Some of the early influences are from my time as a pulpit minister and teacher with Church of Divine Man, and many of the techniques are ones that originated from my experience of that teaching. The pieces from the 1990s take on the flavor of the Sylvan tradition of paganism. Those from the late '90s and into the new millennium add New Thought to my banquet of spiritual bounty. Since writing this book I have also come across Deliberate Creation and the works of Abraham-Hicks and while that isn't specifically included in this work, it is absolutely the form through which much of my life has flowed since discovering it.

The one exception to the period of time mentioned above is the poem titled "The Promise" that begins the last section of this book. This piece is an example of some of the earliest of my work and was written in 1976. I have included it because it was not only profound for me at that time, but has actually made more and more sense as the years have progressed (speaking now 30+ years later). The poem came to me when I was on a seven day hike in the Olympic Peninsula. I had spent 3 days backpacking in, and I had reached my destination, a place called "Home Sweet Home." Later that night, as I was sitting in front of my tent on the side of a mountain under the light of a beautiful and bright full moon in Aquarius, the words started to form in my mind, and I wrote them in the notebook I had carried with me. I was 17. It was years before I had done any of this work or even knew how important roses would become to me spiritually.

I have always loved multiple methods of interacting with the Divine. I have and hopefully will continue to expand my base of experience to include different methodologies, and continue to incorporate these into my personal and professional practice.

I invite you to practice the techniques outlined in this book. Open yourself to the ideas. Dance with them a while, and keep the ones that work for you. All of these concepts are much older than I, although I have packaged them in my own particular verbiage and perspective. Let this book be an opening to remember those things you have always known as Spirit, and to integrate them into conscious awareness. We truly are all One, and so all of these ideas belong to the One and therefore also belong to you.

This is a time in the world and our spiritual evolution as humans when our awareness of the similarities and our Oneness is of utmost importance. I offer this book as one avenue of discovery into the Divine Mystery and connection to All That Is. Know that you are truly loved no matter what your history or condition.

Aloha and blessings,
Erika Ginnis
October 2009

Acknowledgments

I want to thank all the staff past and present of *Widdershins* for prodding me to commit these techniques to writing, for publishing my articles, and for giving me deadlines over the years. Without you this book might never have come to be. From this amazing group of people I want to single out my editor Melanie Henry for her awesome skills and for keeping me to task for so very long, and the publisher Sylvana Silverwitch for being a dear incredibly supportive friend.

I also want to thank The Church of Divine Man, for introducing me to many of these techniques for the first time, the late Rt. Rev. Doc Slusher, and the gifted psychic and teacher Rt. Rev. Mary Ellen Flora who taught me well and who in her absence became wiser (as I got older and I started to finally understand a bit of what she was saying to me when I was in my twenties), and for always validating that I would be a writer.

I also want to thank and hold all the Sylvan Grove and the Green Star Grove in my arms; my brothers and sisters in the craft who have become my family, as we have weaved energy and worked magick together over the years.

The Center for Spiritual Living in Seattle, Rev. Dr. Kathianne Lewis who was always an inspiration to me and helped me to see church and community, and therefore myself, in a totally new way.

The Center for Spiritual Living East Hawaii 'Ohana and The Peace River Choir for being so amazing and welcoming me with open arms, and for my noon-time Nanawale friends, you all truly embody the spirit of Aloha.

All my appreciation for Colette, Elaine, Rebecca, Hank (R.I.P.), Eric Des O'del and all the CSL Choir of Light members past and present whom I sang with throughout the early writing of this book and whose music, love, and light held me up time and time again. I want to thank my group of friends over in Ballard for helping me stay on track, especially Jennie who has been such an amazing friend and confidant. I also want to thank the CSPC, just for being, and for encouraging people to love themselves, for Corinna Hartmann who I found at exactly the right time, and whose councel I treasure.

I want to thank my mom Beverly for living long enough for us to finally know and love each other, for my dad who is helping from the other side. I want to thank my other mom Inez for being with me in spirit all these years, and for being in my life now. I love both my mothers for the countless gifts they have given me.

I want to acknowledge my husband Sam, for his willingness to proofread, for walking next to me through all these amazing journeys, for following the call when you heard it, for so many nights of fires and stories, for all your Virgo ways and for asking me how the book was going often enough that I couldn't ignore it. I love you!

A huge thank you to my dear friend, the amazing artist Bev Rumsey who painted the original cover art. Spirit moved me to Hawaii to find you so I could finish this book! You bless me.

I want to acknowledge the work of Jerry and Esther Hicks and Abraham. Even though I didn't find you until after I wrote the material for this book, you are somehow still in these pages. You are a source of great joy to me. Your wisdom and love are profound, and some of the best stuff on the planet in my opinion.

My love to Amanda, Robbie, Harold, Melanie, Leanne, Adrian Amadeus, Roger, Freya, Russell, Paige, Amy, Simba, China, Saffire, Mark Jones, The late Dr. Bill Mitchell, for always calling me Reverend and treating me as a peer even in yoga class.

Rebecca, Yvonne and the flow of water yoga, Susan DuMett, Michelle Burbridge, Kim Hansen, Rowena, Lucy, Laura Gray, Chuck, Irene, Franny, Lori, Ray, Mike, Mike Jr., Rick, Blackcat, Jimbo, Gina, Mel, Jake, J.T., Marcus Ryan, Heather, Amelia, Liam, Gabriel, and my Goddess daughter Madeline.

I especially want to thank all my clients past and present, you have all been an inspiration to me and taught me so much more than I ever thought possible about spirit and love and joy. I am so blessed to have you in my life. Your presence allows me to do that which I love. I also send my love to all my friends in Seattle and Tacoma, and my friends and on the Big Island of Hawaii where I now live. Mahalo Nui Loa.

In writing these acknowledgments I realize it's possible that I may not have room for everyone since there are so many to name, if you fall into that category just know it is just a typo and that you are in my heart even if your name isn't on this page.

Introduction

The "Play Dough Shape" Theory of Reality

Though this is one of the first ideas I present in this book, it was one of the last ones to make it to paper. I wasn't even going to add this particular idea, but it kept tugging at my sleeve. I realized that it wanted to be in this book. I think it makes a good introduction.

You may have heard the phrase "You create your reality." I know I have heard it a hundred times. For a long time, I wondered what it meant and how it could be. At times, I felt the idea was empowering, at times frustrating and defeating. I thought it meant that if my life was going poorly I was at fault, since I was somehow creating it. However, beating oneself up like that when things are going badly just adds to the pain, which doesn't help at all! Doing that is not what I am talking about here.

Some say it isn't about *what happens* but how you *respond* to it that makes the difference in life. Let's also say that you not only get to create how you respond to your reality, but also by some process you co-create the actual reality itself. Let's go with the idea that reality is way more malleable than we have any concept of, and that somehow you (as spirit) create what shape it comes in, in your life.

How would you and I be doing this? I believe that you create your reality through your beliefs. Your beliefs, whether conscious or not (very often not), are what instruct your thoughts, energy and actions. They influence what you see and how you see it. In fact, they do this so strongly as to make it appear as if what you are seeing is the one and only way anything could exist in "your world" or even "the World." This then is what is called our paradigm. It is our vision of what is real, our structure of beliefs. One of my yoga teachers once said that our paradigm is like a big box or circle drawn around us; we think that the end of this box is the extent of what's possible.

At some point, we make a change or experience something that shifts this ending point. All of a sudden our box breaks open, and it looks as if there are no edges. It can feel scary, and we can feel unsure of what we are doing; this is being out of our comfort zone. In reality, what we have done is expanded our idea of what is possible. As we grow and learn, we become more comfortable and able to use the concepts in this new paradigm. That process will continue until we make another quantum leap to the next level and the next. This is one way that we evolve as people and as spirit.

Why do I bring this up, you might ask, and what does it have to do with play dough? I bring this up because we often want to find ways of changing our reality to better match our dreams and visions. We want more or better ways to expand past our ideas of limitation. (I believe that spirit is limitless and so we as spirit are also.) This book is something that can help you do that. Additionally, I have found that if we can conceptualize something, find something to relate it to, it can make the entire process of shifting and changing much easier. This is where the dough comes into play.

For those of you who haven't interacted with play dough, it is a toy that I played with as a child and still use in my meditation classes. It is essentially a mixture of salt and flour and water that you can press into various shapes. It comes in different colors and is easy to mold. You keep it in a tin so that it remains pliable, and you can use it over and over again. We're getting very spiritual here, can't you tell?

One of the things that you can do with play dough is to use plastic shapes (much like cookie cutters) and press the play dough through the shapes and get stars and moons or squares. It recently occurred to me that this is a fabulous analogy for how we create our reality.

If you have a play dough shape for a star, then whenever you press your play dough through the play dough shape, you will get a star. The play dough doesn't (to my knowledge) have much opinion of the fact that it is now shaped like a star. No matter how many times you take this same play dough and press it through the star shape, you will get a star. If you take a different color of play dough, or get some from your best friend, or buy some that is brand new, if you press it through the plastic that is shaped like a star… you will get a star.

It isn't the fault of the play dough; it is about the mold. It isn't even *your* fault; you are using the shape you have in front of you. It just happens to be the shape of a star.

Let's now say that you are tired of stars, even though they are a great shape. You want something else, like a square. You tell yourself that you are now going to have a square; you take your play dough and confidently press it through the plastic star shape. You get a star. You get sad or frustrated or angry; you try again.

You start to look around yourself, and you notice everywhere around you are these star shapes. It starts to become normal, and it looks like that is just the way things are shaped. Everything you do confirms it; you can make an affirmation or stand on your head under the full moon, and you are still surrounded by star shapes. You decide that stars are fine, you don't even want other shapes, in fact there probably *aren't* any other shapes anyway. If there are, they are probably just stars in disguise.

Perhaps you plead with the powers that be to send you a square; you start to feel that the play dough has it out for you, that maybe you are destined to never have a square, or that it is the will of the Universe that you be forever "square-less". Perhaps you think that it is because of your parents or your spouse or your location. So you get a divorce and move across the country, taking your play dough shape with you.

Guess what? Yep, you're settled into your new home, and as soon as you press some play dough through the mold… you have yourself another star. Why? Because you took your shape *with* you.

What if you suddenly realized that you have a whole additional stack of shapes. They came with the set, but you just never saw them in the box. All you have to do is to put away the shape that makes stars and replace it with one that makes squares. Ha! There among all the stars is your brand new square. Wow! All of a sudden you are free to make play dough into all kinds of shapes. Squares, circles, hearts, and yes, even stars. This may sound like a silly story. But it is an interesting analogy for how we work with universal energy.

The Universe is always saying yes to our beliefs. Through it is an unlimited unending flow of Source. We are all One, and the creative energy of the Universe is available and delights in the ability to show up as a multitude of people, things, plants species and ideas, not so very different from sparkly play dough. It is all about the thoughts, the beliefs, the ideas that filter what that energy flows through. It is like the play dough shape in your head! Some call it pictures, some call it your unconscious myths, some call it your mental equivalent (what you create as normal for you) or your paradigm. Whatever term you use, the good news is, you can identify shapes that no longer serve you and find ways to change them. As soon as you change the plastic shape, the play dough will come out in a different form. Change your beliefs, and reality will look different. You get to consciously pick the shape, and if you don't like it, you can change it. There are a lot of ways to change your play dough shapes. This book shows a few of them. That is one reason I wrote it. I wanted to share some simple ways that I have found to change or expand your experience of reality and embrace a greater yet-to-be for yourself and for this planet.

Section One

Basic Techniques to Begin Meditation

Walk with me

Walk with me
though the destination is a Mystery
Your presence is a joy that quickens my pace
and lightens my step

Walk with me
let the strength of our hands meet
in the center of this journey
warm and real
ordinary as our next breath
and just as miraculous

Walk with me
on this well-worn, but unmarked road
where the Way
is not measured in miles
but in the unfolding of resonant hearts

I could not ask for better company

—Erika Ginnis 1997

CHAPTER 1

Learning to Follow Your Call

This first chapter is about following your call and knowing who you are, but it could easily be about any number of things—perseverance, commitment, focus, following your dream—because, in a way, it is about all these things. We each have a unique purpose in this lifetime, something that we as spiritual beings came here to do. We each have a calling, something we are drawn to, a way in which we seek to learn and explore our creative potential.

Every being's call is individual and may express itself in a variety of ways. We are each a slightly different vibration in the All That Is, a different expression of Deity. And as we are such, there is no one else anywhere who can bring our vibration into the world. I think of it as an orchestra; each instrument is different, but when you put them together you get an incredibly beautiful and complex musical performance. Every violin is played separately, but when you put them together they produce a full chorus of sound, which is different from that of harps, oboes or French horns. A symphony wouldn't sound complete if it were played on only one type of instrument. Or you can think of it as voices in a choir, each voice adding a tone or note to create a chord that rings out and is more than the sum of the parts. Each individual creation is important.

Now, it's very likely that you have been taught to hide or downplay your individuality, being shown that different meant bad, needing to be the same to be part of a group, either at home or perhaps at school. It's very possible that your call was something that you were taught to ignore. Maybe you had a call to the arts and were taught that business was more appropriate, or perhaps business was what you excelled at, but you were taught that science was the most productive path.

So often, we learn that the body and all the material things like money, possessions and security are the only things that are important, or real for that matter. If we focus on the purely physical, it's easy for our own personal spiritual call to become faint, almost drowned out by the worries and needs and the force of the world all around us. Have you ever found yourself wondering: Why am I here? What is my path or tradition? Perhaps you've even looked to others to tell you what was right.

I believe that all we each have to do is to quiet the noise of all that goes on around us and within us, turn within, ask ourselves the question and then listen.

We each have a call, a purpose, a way to follow. We simply need to take the time to listen and hear it for ourselves. That is where perseverance and focus come in. Since it takes faith and focus to follow your calling, whatever it is, it also takes courage and strength. There is always the pull of our own fears and doubts, images of what's "right," things that we have been taught are "essential for happiness" by our upbringing, our church or the advertising media. The act of simply sitting down to communicate with yourself as spirit, and with your source, whether that be the God and Goddess, the Tao, the Universe, the Great Spirit or some other expression, may end up at the end of a very long "to do" list. It can be easy to lose ourselves as spirit in the loud din of this modern world if we don't take the time to stop, turn within, listen and remember who we are.

So who are we? As a working psychic and spiritual teacher, I find in my experience that we are spirit, we are light, each a unique spark of the God and Goddess, an amazing creative expression of infinite possibility.

As we express our individual light, it is like lighting a candle. It illuminates all that is around and in us. Bringing our awareness of ourselves as spirit into the body brings our energy into the body. As we focus, work and learn, we illuminate all that is within us, and the more light that you bring into the body, the more you can see. You naturally develop your clairvoyant (clear-seeing) ability. I believe that we are all psychic. Psychic can be translated to mean "spirit." It is just a matter of putting your attention on it and developing it.

Many people are interested in this, but there are challenges to this kind of work. I have seen many people have a lot of enthusiasm in the beginning, only to falter later on. One of two things can easily happen:

- ✧ Things start to really work great, and whatever malady originally got the person's attention is now gone, so he or she figures there is no need to continue the practice.

- ✧ Things start changing, and get uncomfortable for a while. So the person decides it isn't really working and gives it all up.

I will address the latter of the two examples with an analogy. As I said before, as we come into the body there is more light to see by. As we look around at all that is stored in our body, we may find things that we don't like very much. It's kind of like opening the door to an unused room and turning on the light and seeing all the old furniture and clothes, dust, cobwebs and crumbs there. Maybe, as we look around, we see some things that we had forgotten about or had wanted to hide. It is possible that as we look into this room, peeking in from the door, we wonder why we turned on the light at all—so much cleaning to do!

This is the point at which a lot of people decide to walk away: to quit the practice, to give up on their call, to stop experiencing their own ability to see. We get caught in judgment. This, in my opinion, is the very time to keep going. It is at this point that change can actually begin.

I believe that we are spirit. We are not our body or our creations. We are each a unique bright creative spark of the God and Goddess, divinity incarnate. We as spirit are the light that illuminates the body, our creation. Going back to the room analogy, we are not the room or the things we have stored in it, but the room and all it contains are our creation. We each have a choice, since there is free will, to begin to illuminate, to become "enlightened," to even enjoy and have fun with the process, or to walk away. But whether we chose to deal with it or not, the room (our body) is still our responsibility and will be for the remainder of this life.

Perhaps you have decided that you want to bring that light of you as spirit into your body. You begin a practice; you begin to turn your awareness within to experience yourself and your power. And, as you do this, you are faced with what seems like a daunting task. Sometimes it can obscure the beauty of your creation, but as you make that decision to begin the process of owning and clearing and using that beautiful body (your room, so to speak), you begin to find some space to move around. It can simply be a project, something that takes time and space. One step at a time, but as a process, a learning, you find that you can allow yourself some amusement as you toss out the 20-year-old magazines you have been keeping.

Until you allow yourself to be there and start that process, you keep yourself from all the joy, learning and creativity that is possible, which you actually went to a lot of trouble to put together.

We have each stored unpleasant energy in our bodies, had experiences that were far from pleasant, in this life and in others, which we may not even remember. As soon as we bring in that illumination, we begin to see all of it, pleasant and unpleasant, the things we want to keep and the things we want to release. That just ends up being the process of healing. It is a process we are all in: learning to balance spirit and body.

My point is that it takes time and that's okay. As you learn and grow into your craft, you can begin to love and appreciate this room, workshop, temple, your body, fill it with you. Know yourself as the amazing expression of Deity that you are! And as you do that, you will shine and attract others who are interested in that healing process themselves. You don't have to be done with the project! Simply being there and allowing your divinity will remind others of who they are and that it is possible to heal yourself.

Sometimes it seems easier not to open the door, to ignore our home in this physical reality. But then we keep ourselves from accomplishing all that we came here to do. And that brings me back to where I started. You have a calling. When you allow yourself to be there working with your body, you can hear the sound of your call. You can have the strength and vision to follow it. There is the abundance and harvest and joy that come from hearing your call as spirit and responding.

By following your dream, no matter what it might be, you bring forth to yourself and to this planet more than you could ever imagine.

CHAPTER 2

Grounding

My goal in this and the next few chapters is to put in print some simple energy working techniques that I have learned and taught over the years in my own practice. These techniques are not bound to any one tradition, pantheon or spiritual path. I have seen them used in a number of different circumstances with very positive results. Take them and add them to your tool kit if you like them, or leave them if you don't. However you respond to them, remember: As with any magical or energy working tools, they will only work for you if you actually practice them.

I am going to present the ideas in a specific order because I have found the techniques work best when they build on one another. Some of these tools will be second nature to many of you, and to some they will be a different twist on an old favorite. There are many, many great techniques out there, and these are just a few that I enjoy. I will offer possibilities; use them as a springboard. It is my hope that these techniques will add joy to your life, become a new doorway to your inner self, and that they will assist you to become more aware and present in your magical and spiritual work.

Grounding

Grounding is usually the first technique that I teach anyone. It is the foundation upon which everything else is built. It is very simple and very powerful. I also think it is extremely important. I imagine that many of you have heard of grounding or have practiced it in some way. Most of the rituals and events that I have attended use this technique in some form. Since there are various ways to ground, let me start with some explanation about what I mean when I say "grounding."

Grounding is the act of consciously creating an energy connection as spirit (sometimes visualized as a cord) into and through your body into physical reality/Mother Earth. Grounding brings your spiritual awareness into your body; it connects you into this reality, where you are living and creating. It allows you to have clear access to your own power and energy and your oneness with the Universal source.

You are a spiritual being, and by your nature have a great deal of power and energy. Your vibration is rapid and can be intense. You have a body (yippee!), which is an expression of you that exists in mundane reality, but since it is made of matter, the energy moves at a slower vibratory rate. (Hmm, this sounds like a public television physics program!) When you bring your spiritual energy into the physical body more fully, it can be quite a shock to the system.

Grounding helps keep the body (your sacred temple) a safe place for you to inhabit and experience life through, and prevents it from becoming overly stressed. It helps to keep your energy system safe when you begin to be more fully present in your life. It also helps a great deal when doing any kind of spiritual, meditative or magical working in general. It acts kind of like an electrical ground—it keeps you from getting zapped by an overload of energy. The act of grounding also brings power to your work because it aligns you as spirit with your physical body, so that you can be present and attend to what needs to be done. In addition, it increases spiritual and energetic awareness. It allows you to be senior in your own energy space. Another way to say that is you get to be the executive and make the decisions, responding rather than reacting based on past habits fears or beliefs.

Since grounding brings you present as spirit, you are able to know your own path, feel how you are feeling and be in alignment with your own energy regardless of the activity around you in the world. You can be in the world but not totally affected by it. In this way, grounding is like having a balloon on a string. If the wind blows, your balloon may move around some, but if you are holding the string (your grounding) your balloon isn't going far. However, if you have a balloon without a string and the wind blows, you may be chasing it down the street!

One of the most important aspects of grounding is that it allows you to release energy.

Have you ever been at an event of spiritual and energetic power, a ritual or workshop, perhaps a concert, and felt slightly nauseated afterward or had a headache? Many times, this is a reaction of the body to more intense energy moving through it and not having a way to shunt off the excess flow.

Grounding is a great way to release energy! When you ground, you release unwanted or excess energy, and it gets transformed within this amazing living planet, our Mother Earth, and returns to you renewed. You can release anything down your grounding: people, places, things, experiences, thoughts, emotions. Everything is energy and can be released. When you let excess energy go down your grounding, you benefit everything. You get your own power back, and the energy released is able to return to where it belongs, renewed and refreshed. It reminds me of recycling in a way; you let go of what you are done with, and you get it back transformed. Also, if you are releasing someone else's energy that you took on for some reason, that energy gets returned to that person. It works out well all around.

It is my opinion that the whole energy system of Earth (which I see as our larger body, our sacred mother) is set up to run in this way. We may label what we are releasing as "negative energy" but once we release it from ourselves, to the center of the earth, it is simply energy and becomes part of the flow. I believe it to be a connecting web of moving and shifting energy, of which we are meant to be a balanced part. I also feel that as more people remember and use their grounding, it will begin to revitalize the whole system as the energy begins to flow again.

It might be tempting to think that the only energy you would want to release would be tension or something unpleasant. However, letting yourself ground when running enjoyable energy is just as important. It can be just as difficult to be comfortable in your body with an excess of joy as it can be with an excess of anything else. Plus, higher vibrations need even more grounding. Grounding will let you be comfortable and allow more good to flow to you in your life, since you will be able to handle the energy.

Grounding is also not just for when you want to be "here." I have found grounding to be an essential part of any kind of work, especially that which requires you to journey out of your body, such as path-working, dream work or other kinds of out-of-body work. Grounding in this sense keeps your body safe, comfortable and able to process what you are doing, so it won't pull at you to come back and attend to it every five minutes.

I have spoken about grounding as it relates to spiritual activities, but I want to emphasize that you can be grounded anytime. I highly recommend grounding while playing, eating, making love, shopping, working, driving and so on, as well as during ritual or while meditating. Grounding brings you more fully present and conscious in your life, so that you can respond to situations rather than reacting from past experiences. It will enhance whatever you are experiencing, assist you to be aware of your path and also assist you to move through uncomfortable times more rapidly.

People sometimes notice when they ground for the first time that they become aware of aches or pains they could swear weren't there moments before. The reason for this is simple, if you think about it. If you come into the body more fully, you are going to start to become aware of what your body is actually feeling. If you spend most of your time with your mind in fantasy or off in the future somewhere, you aren't going to be very present to what your body is going through. The minute you ground, though, you align with the body and begin to tune in to what's actually going on.

You might ask why anyone would want to feel tightness in their shoulders if they didn't have to. My answer is this: If you know what is happening and know how you feel, you can begin to take steps to release and heal whatever is causing the problem. The body has much wisdom to teach us if we will but listen. If you ignore the body, it will get louder and louder in an effort to get your attention. I see many people who have begun their spiritual work because some physical ailment caused them to stop and pay attention. You do not have to wait; you can begin the process before being "forced" to by circumstance.

The good news is: When you are grounded, things that are pleasurable are even more pleasurable. You also begin to raise the vibration in the body by grounding it and being more consciously present in it; this will allow an even greater capacity for experiencing the wonders of this planet. It will in turn increase your power and awareness, making you more effective in where you choose to direct your energy.

One of the examples I give my classes is this: Think of all the different books and techniques out there, all the things you can do, as being like a great wall of expensive stereo equipment. It has all the bells and whistles, the CD player and the DVR and the cool speakers. It looks great there on the wall, but none of it will do you a bit of good if you don't plug it in! It really doesn't matter how much you acquire, how many components you buy, if you can't access it. It will just collect dust. Grounding is analogous to taking the power cord and plugging it into the outlet. Then you can use the system. Grounding gives you a way to access your power, because it brings you as spirit (which is the power source) into the picture. None of the techniques will do you much good if you aren't grounded.

There are many good ways to ground. I will not touch on all of them by any means. I will pass on to you one form of grounding I personally use and enjoy. I hope you enjoy it as well. I teach grounding from the first chakra because that is the energy center that relates to physical reality. The first chakra contains information on how to survive and thrive in this reality, and since this is where we have our physical experience and where we want our healing and magic to manifest, I have found grounding from the first chakra to be a sound practice.

Enjoy your exploration with connecting into this planet by grounding. Remember, as with anything, that the experience will change with time. Bring your willingness to explore, allow yourself to be open to your own deepening awareness.

Technique

- Sit comfortably in a straight-backed chair or on the couch (as long as you don't tend to nod off to sleep). Have your hands and feet apart and feet flat on the floor.

- Close your eyes (this helps you to focus inward).

- Take three nice deep breaths, breathe down into your belly and soften your belly as you breathe. It can be helpful (although it is not essential) to breathe through the nose, while keeping your tongue resting lightly on the roof of your mouth. This practice is from certain yoga traditions and is said to help encourage the flow of energy through your system.

- Relax as you breathe, noticing how you feel, how your body feels.

- Be aware of your first chakra. This is simply an energy center (vortex) that is located in the general area near the base of the spine. For women, the center is usually near the area between the ovaries (the chakra positioning doesn't change if you have had your ovaries removed for any reason). For men, the location is slightly lower in the body, because the chakra placement is associated with the testicles.

- Be aware of this area, and allow a cord of energy to flow downward from your body, through the chair you are sitting in, through the floor and down through the building you are in, through the foundation and into the deep earth beneath. Allow your grounding to flow down into the earth past all the rocks and layers of the planet, past the water, deep, deep into the earth, into the heart of the Mother, until it reaches the center of the Earth.

- Allow your grounding cord to connect securely into the center of the planet. Be aware of your grounding cord being securely connected also to your first chakra.

- Breathe and relax and experience your grounding, your spiritual connection to this beautiful planet. Give yourself time.

- Notice how your body responds to your grounding and becoming more present in it. Release tension and discomfort down your grounding; allow it to simply drain away.

- Your grounding belongs to you, and you can create it in any form you like.

- Change your grounding into a waterfall, flowing and cascading from your first chakra down through all of physical reality to the center of the earth.

- Experience this. Take your time. Release and relax; breathe.

- Next, change your grounding into the supple and strong root of a tree, allowing it to grow from your first chakra to the center of the earth.

- Notice how this changes your experience. Breathe. Enjoy.

- Now shift your grounding so that it is a laser beam of light, shining though everything straight down to the center of the Earth.

- How does this feel? Be with this for a moment or two. (Remember you can use any of these groundings at any time; they are simply different ways to experience this connection.)

- Change your grounding once again. This time create your own grounding, flowing from your first chakra to the center of the earth. It can be any one of the three you used before, or something completely unique; it's up to you. This is your very own grounding.

- Use your breath and release down your grounding cord any tension, distractions or discomfort. Notice how you feel as you do this.

- Be still, as you ground and relax. If you have questions, this is the time to ask and listen for the answers. Or simply allow yourself to be.

- It's useful to update your grounding now and then. To do this, simply release it and recreate it, allowing it to be whatever you need for the present moment. This is amusingly similar to upgrading a computer. As you need to process more energy (which happens as you meditate and work with your energy), you need more processing power (more grounding). It's very simple. Say to yourself internally, I am letting my grounding be right in present time, right in the here and now, current for all that I need.

- When you are done, open your eyes, bend forward and touch your hands to the floor, as you relax your neck, and release any built-up energy around the head and shoulders into the earth. Slowly sit back up. If you journal, this would be a great time to record your experience. If not, then you're ready to go on to the rest of your day or evening.

CHAPTER 3

Centering

The center of your head is a place that you can focus yourself as spirit to work energetically and psychically in the body. Centering here is a technique that brings a great deal of power, neutrality and balance to meditation, magic, reading and other spiritual work, as well as the daily experience of life. This is not the only way to center, and many talented readers do not work in this way. However, I have found it extremely beneficial as a reader and teacher, and it is the second technique I teach after grounding.

Being in the center of your head is a simple concept, as you will see in a minute… simple but not always easy. It can take practice to hang out there more than a few minutes at a time—that's where meditation comes in. The discipline of meditating regularly will give you the ability to choose where to place your attention and the focus to keep it there until you decide otherwise. Any time you invest in this technique will be well-spent.

In my opinion, the ultimate goal is actually to balance centering in the place of neutrality, the center of your head, with centering in your heart. However, most people I have worked with equate the head with analytical faculties and intellect, which is something entirely different, and have not experienced the vastness that is actually present in that sacred neutral place associated with the center of your head. On the reverse side, many people who center in their hearts (the heart chakra, actually, which I will cover in Chapter 6) do not balance that heart-centeredness and therefore have not married their feeling with their vision. Nor do they always have an experience of who they are as spirit in this physical body.

If one has experienced a lot of emotional pain in this lifetime, that pain is often stored in the heart center. When one tries to heal the pain or center there, the heart can be muddy or cloudy or feel odd. In addition, it may not feel safe to be there exclusively, because when we are immersed in our heart center we can be more easily swayed by others' emotions or desires. In fact, many have "cut off" their connection to their heart for protection.

That is also not the answer. We are here in this reality balancing opposites. The marriage of head and heart allows for Wisdom, also referred in spiritual texts as the "Sophia." This then is the actual goal. When we center in the center of the head and regain that direction and recognition of self and who we really are, we can go about the sacred work of healing and releasing whatever we need to from our hearts or anywhere else, and we can maintain that sense of self and connection to All That Is throughout the process. We can then more easily express wisdom as we balance *both* head and heart.

In all of this, the act of centering becomes an important part of our inner work. I will explain centering here in detail at the end of this chapter, but for now take a minute and locate this area, so you have an idea of what I am talking about.

✧ One easy way to locate the center of your head is to first ground and relax (see Chapter 2 for information on grounding). Then place the index finger of one hand on your forehead and the index finger of the other hand above one ear. Close your eyes, and picture imaginary lines extending out from each finger and notice where they intersect. When you have found that area, you can put your hands back down.

✧ Bring your awareness and attention to that area in the center of your head. It is actually farther back than the brow/eye area, which is where many people are taught to focus. If you bring your energy a little farther back in your head, you may find (as I did) that the experience is completely different. This place is the center of your head.

The area is somewhat related to the pineal gland, which Descartes referred to as the "seat of the soul." I was told that one of the functions of this gland is to detect amounts of light so that our body knows what season of the year it is. What this same area in the energy body does is to reflect the light of you as spirit throughout the rest of the body.

The center of your head is your own personal sacred place; you can think of it like the altar of your temple. It is your control tower, the driver's seat. Whatever energy or being or thoughts reside in the center of your head are the ones running the show. This is one reason I always suggest that people clear it out and own it for themselves. It is a very powerful place.

This doesn't mean that you always have to be there. There are many things that can only be learned and processed through "out-of-body" experiences. Dreams, visions and some types of path-working are all done with the attention outside of the body. In my opinion, however, it is even more important to own and use this area when you are doing work out of the body, since you will, no doubt, want to return and find things as you left them rather than finding some strange energy hanging around.

It's also much easier while in the center of your head to get in touch with and work from a place of neutrality and not be so harsh and critical about everything (including yourself). It is one reason that it is a really safe place to focus your energy and attention. You can experience life at close range and still maintain your spiritual perspective on things, which is good, since sometimes we all have lessons that are less than pleasant. If you are centered, you are not so apt to lose yourself and become overwhelmed by the problems and challenges that life can hand you.

And if it happens (never to me of course—I have just read about it in books... yeah, right!) that you do become immersed in your current trials and tribulations, you can find a way to regain some perspective and perhaps even find some amusement about your situation. When we get caught in trying to figure it all out or getting into the judgment of it all, it is oh so easy to get stuck in the energy. The neutrality of that quiet, still, balanced place can really help you to move past whatever hurdle you are facing.

There are whole configurations of energy having to do with reading and seeing that are located in the general area of the head and the sixth chakra. The sixth chakra is an energy center or vortex of energy that flows horizontally from in front of the brow through the head and back beyond it a bit. It is sometimes referred to as the "third eye." When you focus your energy in the center of your head, it starts to awaken and stimulate this entire area and will begin to open up your clairvoyant ability. Clairvoyance is French for "clear seeing" and is the term used to describe the ability that we all have (we may or may not use it, but I am of the opinion that we all have this ability) to perceive or see energy, auras, beings, chakras, energetic pictures and so on.

Many people use this word only to mean "seeing the future." This isn't the definition I personally use. Although divination would certainly come under the heading of clairvoyance, I know many people who use their clear seeing ability to do lots of things that are totally unrelated to future vision.

Practicing being in the center of your head is wonderful preparatory work for psychic reading as well as many other spiritual practices. It conditions you to maintain your spiritual focus. As you get more comfortable there, it will give you clarity of vision. It will also change and expand with time, so remain open to the possibilities you may find there. You can get a clear view of what is and not be so influenced by what you think "should" be. It gives you access to your own neutrality, which I find essential in reading so that:

- You are reading the person in front of you and not you own "stuff."
- You don't take on the energy of the person you are reading.
- You allow the person the space to create and learn in whatever way he or she chooses to.

I have found that when you are working from the center of your head it is much easier to accomplish these things:

- ✧ You see the person clearly and are not so influenced by your emotional responses.

- ✧ You can be aware of what's yours and what's not and keep them separate.

- ✧ You can remember that the person you are reading or working with is spirit, just like you are, and has lessons to learn regardless of your opinion of how he or she is doing it.

When something is simple, it can be easy to discount or to rush past in an effort to get to the "good stuff" that is seen as more advanced. What I have found to be true for me is that there is a depth and richness of experience that comes with time. Even, or perhaps I should say especially, in the simplest of these techniques, there is an uncovering of new levels of discovery that happens as you work with them regularly.

It is also variable. There are days that I draw on the vastness of the universe, knowing that all is really within me and present in the center of my head. And then there are days that it is a struggle just to be in the center of my head and not judge myself and everything to death! We are all human, after all. I have found, though, that the tool of centering has been and continues to be incredibly valuable. It has gotten me through even the most stressful of times.

Technique

- Sit comfortably in a straight-backed chair or on the couch (as long as you don't tend to nod off to sleep). Have your hands and feet apart and feet flat on the floor.

- Close your eyes and turn within.

- Start by grounding, as described in Chapter 2.

- When you are grounded, you can take the next step and center yourself.

- Take a nice deep breath, and bring your awareness into the center of your head. Feel free to use your index fingers to help you to focus there if you wish.

- Notice how your body responds. It might have a reaction to you being centered. Let that reaction simply be; notice it. If you experience any discomfort, release it down your grounding.

- Be aware of what the center of your head is like right now. Is it light? Is it dark? Is it crowded, or empty? Cold or warm, big or small? Are you aware of sensations, sounds, images, scents? Relax and breathe yourself into the center of your head. Get comfortable and begin to own this safe neutral place.

- Continue to use your grounding to release energy from this space so that you can make more room for you to focus there in the present moment.

- Say hello silently to yourself as spirit in the center of your head.

- Recognize and validate the essential you. You may be aware of yourself as a bright light, or you may notice your presence in some other way.

- Enjoy the experience. Be aware of your uniqueness and also your connection to all that is.

- Say hello to your body from the center of your head. Notice your body's response. Take a moment and simply allow yourself to be. Allow time to explore being grounded and centered, releasing energy and gaining awareness.

- When you are done, open your eyes, bend forward and touch your hands to the floor, as you relax your neck and release any built-up energy around the head and shoulders into the earth. Slowly sit back up. If you journal, this would be a great time to record your experience.

CHAPTER 4

Creating and Destroying

Creating and destroying are two seemingly different aspects of what I call the cycle of transformation. That cycle is happening everywhere you look. Even though these two processes appear separate, they are actually both integral parts of one cycle. You can't really create without destroying, and you can't destroy without creating. When you create a beautiful meal, you change and destroy the forms of the food that you started with. When you eat the meal, you destroy the form it was in when you set it on the table. When you digest the food, you destroy it further and you create energy to move your body. It is a cycle of transformation. Nothing is ever actually lost; it is only transformed. But one of the ways that change happens is through the process that looks to us like "creating and destroying."

The seasons are a great example of this cycle of transformation, as are the phases of the moon. But we can get hung up on the words "creating and destroying" and the connotation behind them. Very often we will have strong emotional responses to one or the other end of a set of dichotomies (such as creating and destroying). Perhaps we have pain or criticism about our creativity because we created something as a child that looked great to us but wasn't appreciated by the adults around us. I know for myself I created a "beautiful" picture of trees and houses that I was really proud of. However, my paint brushes had been the flowers in the neighbor's garden and my canvas was their freshly painted white house! Needless to say I didn't get the appreciation I thought I deserved!

Perhaps, somewhere along the line, you decided that what you created had to be perfect in order to have value, or that is wasn't as good as someone else's work, maybe a sibling's or classmate, because they were older or more talented in some way. What sorts of experiences do you have in your memory that may be hindering the flow of your creativity? These ideas can influence us on the physical plane as well as in our magical and spiritual work.

We have touched on creativity; how about the concept of destruction? That can be an incredibly loaded word for some people. Have you learned that destruction was bad or even evil? Did you see people in your life that destroyed unconsciously or randomly and created a fearful situation for you? Or perhaps there was a belief that if you destroyed something there would never be anything to replace it, or that there was something wrong with you if you wanted to end something and move on. Perhaps you even stayed in work or relationship situations much longer than was really healthy simply because you didn't have permission to destroy, let go or change.

Destruction in and of itself is not (in my opinion) a bad thing. Without it there can be no change, no transformation.

I am certainly happy when I destroy the odd mold growing in the forgotten container in my fridge (me? Forget to clean out my vegetable crisper? Never!). If you find you have a lot of trouble with the idea of destruction as a valuable aspect of life, perhaps considering the deciduous trees might help give a more neutral example of this cycle.

In spring, new growth happens, and the little leaves pop out and then grow larger and spread out in the summer. Autumn comes, and the leaves turn beautiful colors and then drop off, fall to the earth and decay, making new soil. The plant then goes dormant and the whole cycle starts again. If the tree had only one set of leaves and never let them go, it wouldn't grow larger it would stagnate and eventually die. How silly we would look if during the fall we spent our time collecting the fallen leaves and tried to tape them back on the branches! How uncomfortable we would be if we were still trying to wear the same size clothing we wore when we were 3 years old.

In order to change, one must be willing to let go. This letting go is a destruction of the old pattern of things. You cannot create without destroying, and you cannot destroy without creating. When you destroy, you create a space for new things to appear, just like the old leaves make room for the new ones to burst forth in the spring. What sorts of experiences do you have in your memory that may be limiting your ability to destroy and make changes in your life? These ideas as well can affect us in our magical and spiritual work.

I have been talking thus far about creating and destroying mostly from a physical perspective. Since the actual purpose of this chapter is to present a technique that you can use to exercise your ability to create and destroy as spirit, I will move on to talk about that. As spiritual beings, we have an innate ability to learn, grow, make change and heal. In other words, we have an inherent ability to create and destroy. We do this in magic quite a bit. When we create an intention for some outcome and then we raise energy and release it out into the universe (so that it will return to us) that is a form of creating and destroying as spirit. When we change our mind about something or open it to include a new idea or concept, it is also the same process.

When we focus on doing this consciously, we begin to take back our power as spirit. We begin to exercise our inner divinity and strength. The tool I use to exercise this ability is called creating and destroying roses. This is a very simple and powerful way to work as spirit to create change and transform energy. I will include a meditation at the end, but for now, let's try it out just to get a sense of what it's about.

- ✧ Take a minute to ground and center, then close your eyes (after you read this of course!) and create a mental image picture of a rose six to eight inches in front of your forehead. Notice it, admire it, breathe and validate your creativity (it is not essential that you "see" it, just that you have an awareness of it). Now destroy the rose; blow it up, let it dissolve or pop it like a bubble, notice how you feel.

- ✧ Breathe and validate your ability to destroy and make change. Become aware of the space you created.

You have just consciously created and destroyed as spirit. Congratulate yourself! This may seem like an extremely simple way to work, and it is, but it is also extremely powerful. I assure you that you can create incredible changes working this way. Every time you create and destroy a rose, you change your energy. You automatically begin to release what no longer serves you and fill it with what does. It happens over time of course but it will happen none the less. I personally have used this technique daily in my meditations since the early 1980's. I am also using it as I write this chapter so I can put my ideas down on paper as clearly as I am able.

I suggest adding the technique of creating and destroying roses to the other meditation techniques that I have already presented in the previous chapters. This is part of a strong foundation of energy work that you can use in many different areas of your life. You can use the technique, as you are grounding and centering, to get your energy moving and begin the process of self-transformation and healing.

You can also use creating and destroying roses to clear specific energy. You can do this in one of two ways; both of them work fine, but people seem to like one or the other better. During your meditation, be aware of some thing that you would like to release. This could be tension, or discomfort, or random thoughts or distractions. Or perhaps it is a situation that is on your mind that you have a lot of energy tied up in. Create and destroy a rose or several roses that represent the thing that you want to release. Doing this will release and neutralize the energy from your space. The other way to do this is to be aware of the thing you want to release. Create a rose out in front of you, and let the energy of this unwanted thing flow out into the rose, then destroy the rose. Repeat this until you start to feel a change.

You can clear most any kind of energy in this manner. One of the great things about this is that when you are creating and destroying a rose for something or someone, you are getting your own power and energy back in a neutral form as well as returning the other person's energy back to them in a neutral form. I mention this because I get asked a lot if putting someone's energy into a rose and destroying the rose harms them in any way. The act of working in this way isn't harmful and in fact actually gives them more of their energy back so that they can have access to it. You can use this for people or situations that are pleasant as well as unpleasant. It unbinds you from the unpleasant ones and creates more room for appreciation in the ones that you do enjoy.

The explanation of why I use the rose in this spiritual practice is an entire chapter in itself. However, I will say that some of reasons that I teach and use the rose as a symbol are:

- ✧ It is a neutral symbol to use. We see the rose everywhere; it gets used so much that it is more neutral than many other symbols and doesn't have as much emotional baggage as they might (such as creating and destroying a cute puppy... eek!). This makes it easy to work with the energy itself and not have it be colored as much by our emotions.

- ✧ It is beautiful.

- ✧ It has a lot of spiritual power as a symbol. I have heard it called the Western version of the lotus.

- ✧ As a spiritual symbol, one of its meanings is the emergence of the spirit and its relationship to the Divine (however you experience it or name it).

- ✧ When you work with this symbol, you get the added benefit of increasing your awareness of that relationship and how it works in your life.

With your eyes closed, go through the following exercise. Don't worry if things aren't as clear as you think they should be, simply let yourself have the concept that you are doing the practice and have patience. The awareness will increase with time.

Technique

- Start by grounding and centering. Check your grounding, and be in the center of your head.
- Take a moment to release any "non-permission to create" down your grounding. Take as long as you like. Breathe and release. Validate your ability to create.
- Release any "non-permission to destroy or to make change", down your grounding. Breathe and release. Own your ability to destroy and transform in ways that are beneficial to you.
- Create a mental image picture of a rose out in front of your forehead about six to eight inches.
- Be aware of your creation—admire it. Release energy down your grounding.
- Destroy the rose. Be aware of your energy; notice how your body responds. Breathe deeply.
- If you have any trouble with either creating or destroying, keep using your grounding to release the energy.
- Begin creating and destroying roses as rapidly or slowly as feels comfortable. Notice how it affects your energy. Be with this for a few minutes to get comfortable with it.
- Start to work with intention by creating and destroying roses to enhance your grounding. Feel this shift in the energy. Breathe.

- Next use creating and destroying roses to clear out more room for you in the center of your head. Breathe and notice this change.

- Now choose something that you would like to release, perhaps tension or distractions. Create and destroy a rose for the thing you want to release. Keep doing this for a while, and notice how you feel.

- Ground and breathe. Bring yourself back to the center of your head if you find you have drifted off.

- Something fun to do is to create a rose out in front of you, and leave it there for a moment. With your eyes closed, take your physical hands and begin to feel the energy of the rose, really touch it and get a sense of what it feels like. It really exists. Breathe and release energy. Put you hands back down. Then destroy the rose. Put your hands back up and feel the space where the rose used to be, notice how this feels. Let yourself feel the space that you just created. Breathe and ground; release energy. Validate that what you are working with is real. Validate yourself as spirit.

- Continue to ground, center, create and destroy roses and let yourself simply be. If you have questions of yourself or the universe, ask them now and then listen for the answers.

- When you are done, open your eyes, bend forward and touch your hands to the floor, as you relax your neck and release any built-up energy around the head and shoulders into the earth. Slowly sit back up. If you journal, you might record your experience. If not, then go on to the rest of your day or evening.

CHAPTER 5

Working with Earth and Cosmic Energy

In this chapter, I am going to talk about and teach a technique for consciously moving energy through your body and energy system. This technique is made up of four sections, which when combined make for a very joyful and powerful practice to increase you own energy, heal yourself and get in touch with your own inner magic.

For the greatest success, I recommend that you review the information given in the previous chapters on grounding, centering, and creating and destroying roses. These techniques provide a good foundation for the next set of exercises.

We all move energy in one way or another. Some people do it consciously; some do not. We raise it when we do rituals, or dance or sing, when we make love or laugh. As long as we live, the energy will flow. It is known by many names, some of which are chi, life force, vital force, earth energy and cosmic energy. We each have the ability to enhance this flow through us to enrich our work and our lives. There are many different systems of working with this energy and many different pathways that it can be directed through.

I personally believe the most important factor is to begin to work with the energy consciously and a less important factor is the form you use (though I obviously have my favorites). Without conscious attention, we have little impact on whether our energy will be more or less vibrant, whether we feel charged up or depleted. We will have little say about healing blockages, which means the energy may flow more slowly and perhaps miss some areas altogether. When we have a conscious practice to intentionally move the universal energies through our bodies, we have a way to renew ourselves and come from a place of fullness rather than depletion. This is very powerful.

I personally believe that we have all that we need somewhere inside of us. I believe that the space within us is actually infinite, that in some indefinable way the universe, the God and Goddess, all we seek, all answers, can all be found within, even as they are simultaneously all around us. As we receive the energies that are always available to us, this allows us to connect with that which is all already inside us. I also have had the experience that unless we find a way to uncover what which is within us, grow into who we are, it will seem all we seek, all we need, is anywhere but where we are. It's one of those "Divine" (grrrr) paradoxes.

When we feel like we don't have a way to tap into that unending supply, it can be quite distressing. We can find ourselves looking for ways to hoard energy (which of course stops the flow). We may only feel good when we are around someone else who has a lot of energy. If we are big healers and givers, we can find ourselves "giving ourselves dry" and then resenting it. It's like having a finite amount of water in a pitcher and having to dole it out sparingly. When we feel like the energy we need to live, grow and thrive is available to us, we live differently. We can use it, allow it to flow freely and give from our abundance, like pouring water from a pitcher that is being constantly filled. The water comes of its own accord because it has to be given; it's overflowing. This isn't to say that we don't have to take the time to recharge ourselves. It is just that we know we can, and that there isn't such a scarcity.

When we work with grounding, centering and creating and destroying roses, we begin to come more into the body and clear unwanted or non-beneficial energy from our psychic/spiritual space. Consciously "running your energy" is one of the ways I use and teach to replenish nourish, inform and vitalize that psychic/spiritual space. Conscious movement of energy can do much more than simply replenish the system, however. It can increase awareness, help to heal blockages, stimulate the chakra system (I will deal with chakras in more depth in another chapter) and balance our energy. Conscious energy movement can create that place between earth and sky where we as spirit can harmoniously dance in and through our physical selves.

This practice can and usually does create change and stimulate growth in us as well. It can sometimes stir up old experiences, energies or blocks that need clearing, and you might find yourself at some point feeling very uncomfortable. It is important to remember that this is part of the process, and not to stop the work. One of my former teachers used to use the old adage "When you are up to your ass in alligators, it's hard to remember you set out to drain the swamp." It took me a long time to understand what she meant by that, but I eventually got it!

I like to think of it as being like going out into your backyard in the spring and deciding to clean out the old cement pond that has been sitting there for perhaps many years. When you look at the pond, it has water in it that is pretty clear down to the bottom, where everything has settled and the sediment has formed. The pond looks basically fine, but you know that since it has been sitting for a while, there is some cleaning to be done.

When you start to run water from the hose through the pool, the water immediately turns murky, and up come dead leaves, old toys, water bugs and dirt, along with strange unidentifiable shapes that may at one time have been an apple core or tennis shoe. Yuck! The pond looks really nasty! It may even smell bad. If you stop at this point, it will take a while for everything to settle back into the depths. It will be icky to look at, and you will not have accomplished your task. If you keep running the water through it and keep clearing out the assorted items that you find stirred up, however, you will eventually have a pond that is clean and has clear water all the way down to the bottom. Now if autumn leaves fall into the pond, you will have a much easier time clearing them out. You notice them right away, and it's a pretty specific, doable job.

Running your energy is like clearing out this old pond. The most important thing I can tell you is to keep it up, and not to stop just because something gets uncovered that you don't like much. If you keep up the practice, you will move past whatever it is and get to places within yourself that you never knew were there.

The way I teach to consciously move your energy is to work with the energies of the earth and sky, the cosmic energy. One of the reasons I chose to write this chapter now is that it is the time that the God and the Goddess come together (no pun intended... really...). It is Beltaine. Yahoo! When we run our own cosmic and earth energies and allow them to blend and flow, it is like being the vessel for that divine union. It is from that dance that all life and change emerges and springs forth.

We can direct energies through our bodies in numerous ways, such as with breath or imagery. There are many fabulous ways to accomplish this; the following is one way to do so. Experiment with it and have fun.

Technique

- Start by grounding and centering.

Earth Energy

- While keeping your attention focused in the center of your head, be aware of your feet. Silently say hello to them. Allow the energy of the planet (earth energy) to begin to gently flow into the arches of your feet. Feel it as it flows up through your feet, and then moves slowly into your calves and thighs. Relax and feel this flow of energy; it may be warm or cool, or it may be simply an awareness.

- Let the energy flow into your hips and then move through that area called the first chakra (located near the base of your spine if you are male, or between the ovaries, if you are female) and then flow back down your grounding. This flow of energy will strengthen your grounding and cleanse it as it flows. These pathways from the arches of your feet through your legs into your first chakra, where it connects into your grounding, are called your leg channels or earth energy channels.

- Notice how the energy moves like a circuit, up through the feet, moving though your leg channels, flowing into the first chakra, and then down your grounding. This is earth energy, the energy of the planet. It is the energy that our bodies are made from.

- It is a very powerful and validating energy for our bodies to experience. It can be very healing when we consciously move it through the leg channels in a gentle and cleansing manner.

- Take a moment and simply allow your experience to unfold. Breathe. Once you have this energy moving, simply let it be, and it will move on its own.

Cosmic Energy

- Check your grounding, and refocus in the center of your head. Allow your earth energy to continue its flow. Be aware of the top of your head. Create a bright ball of cosmic (sky) energy above your head; allow it to be like bright, warm, golden sunlight. This is the energy that emanates from the cosmos; it is unlimited and always available. It has many vibrations; gold is one that I particularly enjoy and recommend working with.

- Allow this bright energy to gently flow into the top of your head and flow down either side of your spine to your first chakra. These pathways from the top of your head and down the sides of your spine to the first chakra are called your cosmic energy channels or back channels.

- Experience your cosmic energy; allow it to melt away tension or blocks. When you allow your cosmic energy to run, it will automatically begin to increase the vibration of the physical body. This is a process of "waking up" the body, and it in turn makes it easier to more fully experience your spiritual/psychic awareness. Breathe and relax.

Blending of Energies

- Making sure you are still grounded and centered, notice how your earth and cosmic energies, as they flow, meet in your first chakra. Allow this meeting of energies to be a dance, a blending or your own unique mixture of earth and sky—your own divine union. Allow this blend of energies to begin to move gently up the front of your body and out the top of your head like a fountain. These pathways from the first chakra up both sides of the front of the body and out the top of your head are called your front channels.

- Experience this blend of energies; allow this flow to gently wash away any blocks or tension. Feel it as it fountains out the top of your head and flows all around your body, eventually flowing down your grounding.

Healing and Creative Energy

- Finally, as you breathe and relax, allow some of the energy that is flowing up your front channels to branch at the cleft of your throat and flow down your arms and out your hands. These pathways from the cleft of the throat, down the arms and out the chakras in the palms of the hands are called your healing and creative channels.

- Feel this energy as it flows out your hands. This is the energy you use to make changes and heal yourself and others, as well as the energy you use to manifest your spiritual creativity in physical reality. Tune into your healing and creative energy. Breathe, release energy down your grounding, relax and be in the center of your head.

- Let all your energies flow at once. You don't have to "try" to make any of them move; simply relax and notice them, and they will move on their own. Validate yourself. You are releasing, energizing and healing, simultaneously and effortlessly. If you want to enhance your work further, you can add creating and destroying roses as you run your energy. This is the foundation and the heart of all the meditation work that I personally do and teach. Give yourself permission to work with this and practice, even if it feels odd at first. It will unfold greatly over time. If you have questions of yourself or the universe, ask them now, and then listen for the answers.

- When you are done, open your eyes, bend forward and touch your hands to the floor, as you relax your neck and release any built-up energy around the head and shoulders into the earth. Slowly sit back up. If you keep a journal, write down your thoughts. Enjoy.

CHAPTER 6

Chakras

If you have read the last few chapters, you will have learned ways to ground, center, create and destroy roses and also consciously circulate your energy. There are many places I could go from this point, since those basics are the foundation by which you can begin to explore your psychic/spiritual inner world. As I have been thinking about what to focus on next, I keep returning to the topic of chakras.

There is already a great deal of information available on chakras, and most of it is extremely helpful. If you want to really delve into this subject, go to your local bookstore and start reading. My own preference is to keep it simple and work with the actual energy centers themselves, since some of the writings, in my opinion, can get so technical that you can lose the magic of the experience. There is the added problem that since this is such an ancient topic and so much has been written about it that you will find that not all the texts are in agreement.

With that in mind, my intention here will be to give basic information and provide a guide for personal meditations so that you can begin to find out for yourself what kind of treasure is stored within you.

The word chakra I am told is Sanskrit for turning wheel or spinning wheel. A chakra is an energy and information center in the energy body. There are lines of energy that run through the body; anywhere these lines cross, you will find a chakra. This means that there are lots and lots of chakras. There are chakras in your lips, the tips of the fingers, the knees, among some other interesting places. I am however only going to talk about some of the main chakras in this chapter. The main chakras are places where many energy lines come together and create a major vortex of energy and information.

You can think of a chakra as kind of a turning vortex of energy that is roughly funnel or "ice cream cone with the end cut off" shaped. When I teach someone about chakras I usually roll up a piece of paper to give that very esoteric representation of these amazing centers of information. The iris of a camera is another good analogy to the chakra because chakras have the ability to open or close.

Over the years, there have been some inventions that I think parallel chakras very nicely. These didn't exist at all when I started teaching, but I almost always mention them in any chakra discussion I have these days. The inventions I refer to are music CDs and CD-ROMs. I didn't realize the connection until I saw that when you play a CD it spins in the player; the same is true, I have been told, for a CD-ROM in a computer. This is so much like a chakra it's amazing, little discs that you read with light that give you information when you spin them! Pretty cool.

As I mentioned before, chakras have the ability to open and close. I never recommend closing any chakra completely down.

And unless you are very familiar with working with them and have had some training in the subject, I generally recommend that you allow your chakras to automatically adjust to the openness they need to have at any given moment.

I have met some people that are of the opinion that more open a chakra is the better, as if that were the only way to get access to the information. I don't necessarily agree.

My experience has been that you have your own information inside of you and you can get in touch with that quite well without blasting open your chakras. In fact, sometimes what can happen in that situation is that you end up so open to everything outside of yourself that you don't have a clue how you feel or what your own information might be on a given subject.

My suggestion is to learn to work with the energies and really own them for your self and get to know them. Become aware of what is happening, and learn from that. It's too easy to get overwhelmed with the energy and then decide you want to close way down and not deal with it at all. I much prefer to take the time to go at a more relaxed pace and stay in harmony with the body.

There are seven main chakras in the body. The first six run horizontally through the body and the energy (as I teach it) runs through the chakra from the front (the large end of the ice cream cone) to the back (the smaller end of the ice cream cone). The seventh chakra runs vertically as does the energy. There is more exchange of energies within the chakra system, but for the sake of simplicity this is a good place to start.

Whenever you consciously run your energy (as I outlined in the last chapter), you begin to stimulate the chakra system. The front channels that run up the body actually run alongside the chakras. The act of running your energy will begin to increase the rate your chakras spin and increase the movement of energy and information through them.

Many of you out there are very visually oriented and will want to associate color with the chakras. That's fine, of course, but I will add my own take (read soapbox) to the chakra/color correspondence. If you want to make a correspondence between the seven rainbow colors and the seven chakras, it can be a nice meditation. However, I do want to point out that this isn't the same as it being the "ideal" or "standard" color for the various chakras.

Aura vibrations as well as chakra vibrations change all the time based on a great number of factors. I am of the opinion that it is limiting to think that the first chakra has to always be "red" for instance. It could be any color at all or some combination of colors. One of the colors I use a lot, a clear gold, isn't even in the main seven rainbow colors. The closest you can get is yellow, which is a completely different vibration altogether. My point here is to keep your options open and not get too restrictive when it comes to colors. I think that you'll get a lot more out of it that way (she says, stepping off her soapbox).

You have a wealth of information within you. As you begin to own and work with your chakra system, you have the opportunity to get in touch with levels of yourself that you may not have even knew existed. In the chakra meditation that follows, I recommend that you keep releasing energy down your grounding so that you can enjoy your exploration, and that you experience the energy of each chakras while still staying in that safe neutral place called the center of your head. Being grounded and centered will make it easier for you to experience the energies without becoming them. Let it be simple, and have fun.

Technique

- Check your grounding, and be in the center of your head. Begin to run your earth and cosmic energies, as described in Chapter 5, and allow some healing and creative energy to flow down your arms and out your hands. To enhance your work further, you can add creating and destroying roses.

The Chakra Meditation:

First Chakra

- From the center of your head, be aware of your first chakra. It is near the base of the spine, somewhat in front of it. Since the first chakra is associated with the testicles or the ovaries, this chakra is located higher in the female body (between the ovaries) than it is in the male body. This chakra is the energy and information center associated with survival: being in physical reality, dealing with things like jobs and money and living in a body.

- Let yourself breathe and relax and tune into this chakra from the center of your head. Own it. Allow your own energy to flow through it from front to back. Notice what you experience. Release any non-beneficial energy down your grounding.

Second Chakra

- From the center of your head, be aware of your second chakra. This is located a couple finger widths below your navel. It is the energy and information center associated with emotionality and sexuality, clairsentience and gut-level feeling.

- Let yourself breathe and relax and tune into this chakra from the center of your head. Own it. Allow your own energy to flow through it from front to back. Notice what you experience. Release any non-beneficial energy down your grounding.

Third Chakra

- From the center of your head, be aware of your third chakra. This is located at the solar plexus. It is the energy and information center associated with power and energy distribution. It also has to do with out-of-body experience (dreaming and so on) and memory.

- Let yourself breathe and relax and tune into this chakra from the center of your head. Own it. Allow your own energy to flow through it from front to back. Notice what you experience. Release any non-beneficial energy down your grounding.

Fourth Chakra

- From the center of your head, be aware of your fourth chakra. This is located at your sternum. This is your heart chakra. It is the energy and information center associated with affinity and feelings of oneness and universal connection. Let yourself have some of your own affinity for yourself.

- Let yourself breathe and relax and tune into this chakra from the center of your head. Own it. Allow your own energy to flow through it from front to back. Notice what you experience. Release any non-beneficial energy down your grounding.

Fifth Chakra

- From the center of your head, be aware of your fifth chakra. This is called the throat chakra and is located at the cleft of your throat. It is the energy and information center associated with communication. It is a busy chakra. It has five main aspects:

    ✧ Inner voice (that still small voice within)

    ✧ Clairaudience (which means clear hearing but refers to hearing beings without bodies)

    ✧ Broadband telepathy (telepathic communication over long distances or with large groups)

    ✧ Narrow-band telepathy (communication over short distances or between a few people)

    ✧ Pragmatic intuition (things like knowing who is calling on the phone before you pick it up without having Caller ID)

- Let yourself breathe and relax and tune into this chakra from the center of your head. Own it. Allow your own energy to flow through it from front to back. Notice what you experience. Release any non-beneficial energy down your grounding.

Sixth Chakra

- From the center of your head, be aware of your sixth chakra. This is called the third eye and is located at your brow. It is the energy and information center associated with clairvoyance (which means clear seeing, and has to do with seeing energy). This chakra also has to do with abstract intuition (knowing the answer to a problem without going through the necessary steps) and neutrality.

- Let yourself breathe and relax and tune into this chakra from the center of your head. Own it. Allow your own energy to flow through it from front to back. Notice what you experience. Release any non-beneficial energy down your grounding.

Seventh Chakra

- From the center of your head, be aware of your seventh chakra. This is called the crown chakra. It is located at the top of the head. It is located partially in and partially out of the body. This is the only chakra that runs vertically. It is the energy and information center associated with knowingness and having your own spiritual answers. It also has to do with bringing your spiritual information into the body. It also is associated with trance-mediumship (channeling), as it is the chakra that is sometimes used to leave the body and bring another entity in (something I don't recommend unless it is really your life's work). This is also the only chakra that I recommend allowing to be shaped more like a tube rather than a funnel. It will make it a lot easier to work with, and not to get overwhelmed by an influx of energy.

- Let yourself breathe and relax and tune into this chakra from the center of your head. Own it. Allow your own energy to flow up through it and out the top of your head, and fountain all around you. Notice what you experience. Release any non-beneficial energy down your grounding.

Hand Chakras

- You have chakras in the palms of your hands. They are the chakras that your creative and healing energy flows out of. Let that energy flow and notice it. Release any non-beneficial energy down your grounding.

Foot Chakras

- You also have chakras in the arches of your feet. They are the chakras that allow the energy of the planet to flow into your body. Allow them to relax. They are a set of chakras that it is totally okay to allow to be really open. Let that energy flow and notice it. Release any non-beneficial energy down your grounding.

- When you are done, open your eyes, bend forward and touch your hands to the floor as you relax your neck and release any built-up energy around the head and shoulders into the earth. Slowly sit back up. If you keep a journal, this would be a great time to record your experience. If not, then you're ready to go on to the rest of your day or evening.

CHAPTER 7

Aura and Protection Rose

I am going to talk about a couple of different awareness techniques in this chapter. The main focus is going to be on what I will refer to as your "protection rose," which I will explain in a bit. However, in order to actually teach this technique, I need to first talk about the aura, since these two things are closely linked.

Your aura is an energy field that surrounds your body. It is all around you like an eggshell is around an egg, or like the glow from a candle. Many different people have opinions about what it is made of or what it consists of. I am not going to give a great deal of background along those lines, since there is so much good material already available on this topic.

Your aura is constantly changing depending on what you are doing and what you are experiencing at any given moment. It is your personal, private psychic space. Whatever is going on within you is also being projected in some fashion out into your aura. The energy of the chakras, which I talked about in the last chapter, flow out into and through your aura. This is one of the things that someone looks at when they "read" your aura. They are looking at these same energy patterns. Your aura is the window through which you see the world and through which the world sees you. It affects your perception. It is also your very own sacred space.

I am of the opinion that it is worth as much time and attention as any other sacred space on the planet since, as we learn to treat ourselves with respect, we will bring this into our lives and onto the earth.

Not many of us were taught as children that we had our own space at all, let alone having an aura. You may have given up this idea to some extent at an early age. So this concept may seem foreign to you. Using energy working techniques can assist you to regain that lost awareness. Your personal space is yours, plain and simple. You can chose to give it away, share it, trash it or revel in it, but it is yours for this lifetime.

- ✧ The first step to owning something is of course to know you have it.

- ✧ Take a moment and close your eyes. Let yourself become aware of your body.

- ✧ Let yourself become aware of the energy surrounding your body; notice it above your head and underneath your feet, on both sides of you and all around you.

- ✧ This is your aura. Let yourself have an awareness of the edges of your aura. Notice how far away from your body this extends. You can have your energy extended really big, or pulled in really tight.

- ✧ Play with it a little and notice how it feels. I suggest letting your aura relax and flow to extend it one and a half to two feet or so all around the body. This gives you space and at the same time doesn't encompass any unnecessary energy in your general vicinity. If you have trouble gathering your energy around you, breathe and relax and increase your grounding. (For more on grounding, check Chapter 2.)

Whether you know it or not, your aura is being affected by lots of different energies throughout the day. You may take things on as you go through your day, you may project things outward; it all depends.

Have you ever been around someone who you knew was really angry but it wasn't from their words or their body language? You were probably tuning into the energy that was being projected out into their aura. And if that person had their energy moved out from their body a great distance, you may have been, not only perceiving their energy, you may have been actually experiencing it.

As you become more tuned in to your own energy, by grounding and centering and moving your energy consciously, you may find yourself becoming more sensitive to energy in general. It is also very possible that you have always been sensitive to energy and that is what drew you to energy work in the first place. One of the things that I have found important in my own work is to find a way to be able to have some ability to control how sensitive I am at any given time. When you walk around being sensitive to everything around you, it can be very uncomfortable, to say the least. It can make you want to turn everything down, or find a way to "harden" yourself to the world at large and people in specific. This can be painful to do especially if you are inclined to be a seer or healer in any way.

What I have found to be a much-preferred option is to increase awareness, and not rely on sensitivity as much. This may seem like splitting hairs; however, there is a difference. When you are aware, you can perceive energy without being directly affected by it in the same way you would be if you were "sensitive" to it. You can then have more of a choice as to what kind of energy you want to experience.

I have found this essential when I am working with people in a healing capacity. If I had to "feel" everything they were going through along with them, then I would be of much less assistance to them. Instead of working on healing, I would spend much of the time, either writhing in pain on the floor, running from them, or else trying to control them so that they wouldn't be feeling anything I didn't want to also experience. Sound at all familiar?

As I allow my empathy for their situation to combine with my awareness of the energy around it, I can best see what kind of work to do and do so without taking on the energy into my own aura. I am not saying I do this perfectly, because I don't. That is what grounding and releasing energy is for!

However, having techniques to use to increase awareness and relieve some of the excess sensitivity has been an integral part of my own well-being. In my case, it has actually increased my ability to really relate to people, since I don't have to spend as much time worrying about becoming overwhelmed by them.

I would like to share one of the techniques that I have used for many years that assist in this process. This technique as I mentioned earlier is called the "protection rose." This is a symbol that you create and place at the edge of your aura. It helps you become aware of the edge of where your energy ends and the rest of world begins. It is like a marker. Kind of like having a fence that marks the boundaries of your yard, a protection rose is a marker that announces to you and to the world that you are consciously aware that you are spirit and that you have space.

People will actually respond to this in a big way, even if they don't know what it is to which they are responding. I especially like using it when it feels like someone is trying to push their energy into mine in a way that is unwelcome or is trying to convince me of something (such as when encountering a particularly intense salesperson). I also use it on the freeway a lot when someone is tailgating me. If I put up my rose, almost without fail, the person will move around me or back way off. What I think happens in this case is that the rose surprises the person who has probably been driving on mental automatic, and reminds them that there is indeed another car right in front of them. People respond amazingly well to energy even if they are not consciously aware if it.

I have also known of a few people that have had the experience of someone actually commenting on being aware of the rose and asking, "Why do you have that rose floating out in front of you?" Animals will also be aware of it, and it can be a handy way to create space if you are dealing with an unknown animal, or even a well-known pet that you would like a little more space from (say when you are trying to meditate).

It is also a protection in that it acts as an absorber of energy. If, let's say as in the example above, you are in the company of an angry person and they consciously or unconsciously throw a little energy your way. If you have a protection rose up, that energy will hit the rose first and get diminished somewhat before it affects you. This may of course wear on your rose a lot, but you can easily destroy the old protection rose and create a new one any time you wish. In reality, I always suggest that you check your protection rose periodically to make sure it hasn't gotten destroyed by miscellaneous energy as you go through your day.

It is also very informative to notice your rose when you are in a situation when you think that someone might be throwing energy in an aggressive manner. If you notice your protection rose keeps disappearing, that can be an indication that you are getting some extra attention.

You may be familiar with different ways to shield yourself from energy. The protection rose is not technically a shield. It is really more or a marker, a reminder to yourself and the world that everything from the rose in is you, and everything from the rose outward is not. One of the downsides to shields in general is that they can sometimes attract more energy than they repel, or they can insulate you more completely than you really wish. I am not saying that there aren't times and places where shielding is totally appropriate and extremely useful. However, the benefit of a protection rose is that you can have it up and not attract a ton of attention or isolate yourself, *but* you can keep your sensitivity from overwhelming you, while at the same time gaining awareness in general. I have even seen it assist people who are uncomfortable in social situations, because they feel less "raw" or claustrophobic.

Another way you can benefit from this technique is to use it within intimate relationships to maintain your own sense of selfness, or to create enough space so that you can continue to really see and appreciate the other person. It is also a way to maintain or regain your uniqueness after an intensely bonding experience without having to push the other person away. In addition, it can be very helpful in discussions or even during conflicts with a loved one, so that you have more of a chance to communicate what you are really intending to communicate and still maintain respect and awareness of boundaries.

Lastly the protection rose can be really helpful in maintaining an awareness of your own sacred space. If you want to know where the edge of your aura is you can just look for your protection rose. If you notice it is really teeny tiny, this may be an indication that your aura is way, way out there and this might be the reason you feel overloaded or kind of spacey. This gives you the cue to perhaps draw your energy in around you a bit more. Or if you notice your rose being up against your nose... you might decide that you might like a little more breathing room and relax your space a little. The key here is that you are the one who is now able to respond and choose.

This is a sacred precious place you inhabit. Your body is a temple, and the aura is like the sacred ground that surrounds it and within which it is housed. Let yourself honor this as you would any other sacred place on earth.

Technique

- Start by grounding and centering. Check your grounding, and be in the center of your head.

- Begin to run your earth and cosmic energies, and allow some healing and creative energy to flow down your arms and out your hands. To enhance your work further, you can add creating and destroying roses.

Aura and Protection Rose

- As you allow your energies to run, tune back in to your aura. Be aware of it surrounding your body on all sides, in front of you and behind you and underneath your feet. Notice that the energy fountaining out the top of your head is flowing out and through your aura clearing and cleansing it. Own your aura for yourself; take your hands and run them through this energy field and see what that feels like. Begin to get acquainted with your own energy.

- Keeping your eyes closed, have an awareness of creating a large rose out in front of you. (This will not affect the roses you use when you practice the creating and destroying technique, since this one will float at the edge of your aura.) Let this rose stay at the edge of your aura about face height. This is your protection rose.

- Notice how it feels to be in the center of your head, behind your protection rose, which is at the edge of your aura. How does it make you feel? Let this rose go and make a new one, just so that you have the experience of recreating it. How does the new protection rose feel? Is it easier to feel? Play with expanding and contracting your aura, and notice how this affects the placement of your rose.

- This is a very simple technique, and also very powerful. Give yourself permission to play with it and notice what kind of awareness it gives you. Use your rose in different situations, and see how it changes your experience. Let it be a marker, an announcement to yourself and to the world that you know that you are spirit and that this space around you is yours and is sacred.

- When you are done, open your eyes, bend forward and touch your hands to the floor, as you relax your neck and release any built-up energy around the head and shoulders into the earth. Slowly sit back up. If you journal, this would be a great time to record your experience. If not, then you're ready to go on to the rest of your day or evening.

CHAPTER 8

Corner of the Room

(How to Take a Vacation, Without Leaving Your Home)

I want to relay to you a teaching that is one of the last things I am adding to this book, regardless of where it appears in the chapter order. I always teach it to students, but I wasn't going to add it because it is very experiential and not easily grasped by the mind, since it isn't a *mental* practice. Then one of my clients came to me and said she had searched all my writing on my Web page and couldn't find this technique anywhere. She asked me to write about it, and I took that as a direct request from the Universe.

As you are learning this technique, resist the urge to have it make sense to your body (it won't) or to intellectualize it. There isn't a perfect way to do it; there is only your experience of how it occurs each time you do it. The understanding will come with the experience of practicing it.

Throughout this book, I focus mainly on techniques that can assist you to consciously bring your energy as spirit more into your body and connect into this physical plane. One of the reasons behind getting you into your body in the here and now is that this is really where you chose to incarnate (stood in line to get here). And even if you *didn't* read the fine print on all those great travel brochures that told you all about the cool things to do and see on Earth, you are here. Therefore, some part of your path is about manifesting spirit (you) here (in your body).

It's not that being in your body is "good" and working out of your body is "bad." They are just two different ways of working. In fact, many types of meditations specifically teach ways to detach from this physical world, or do "traveling" out of your body, sometimes called path-working.

Some things can only be effectively done "out of the body." Since spirit is not bounded by time and space, it can do certain things more easily outside of that system. This practice is about balance (we are here balancing dichotomies) and intention—learning ways to consciously choose where your attention will be focused, at any given moment, so you can be at choice about whether you work from inside your body or not.

This technique I am going to describe is called "corner of the room." It is a wonderful way to take a mini-vacation without leaving your own home, plus it's a lot easier on your body than some of the other ways of getting out of the physical plane.

While I recognize that the name might hold some old childhood or school memories that are less than pleasant, I would invite you to simply put them to one side for the duration of this chapter. The practice, as I am going to teach it, is something very different than those others and can be quite fun.

As I mentioned previously, you are spirit, and as such you are not bound by time and space. You can be anywhere or everywhere, and in fact wherever your attention is, there *you* are. This is one reason why paying attention to someone is a high and holy gift. One of the opportunities we have on this plane is to become aware of the power of our attention and further learn how to turn our attention in the direction we want to go. Gathering our scattered awareness is sort of like focusing a diffuse light into a more intense beam, such as a laser. Our ability to consciously direct our attention is important because what we put our attention on tends to increase. The reason why it increases is because once we put our attention on something, we are putting our light into it and adding to it. This is very powerful stuff.

One way to become familiar with consciously shifting your attention, or focus as spirit, is to move into the center of your head. I have already outlined this previously (see Chapter 3). Another way to shift your attention (that is the complement of centering) is to consciously move your awareness outside of your body in a safe and simple way. When I say to move your awareness, I mean *only* that. I am not speaking of trying to move your astral body, or any other body that you may be aware of. I mean moving your energy as spirit, your attention, *you*, and leave all the things associated with your body right where they are.

Oddly enough, this technique can also assist you to be more centered. The more you can get into your body, the more you can get out, and the more you can get out of your body, the more room there is to get back in. It's kind of like going on a vacation that is long enough, and then being able to return to your life more fully present, because you are refreshed and interested again. The difference is, with going to the corner of the room you don't have to buy tickets and you can do it in the space of a very few minutes.

Always ground and center (see chapters 2 and 3) before starting this technique. Grounding and centering connects you to this plane and helps you to be safe and feel comfortable. Also, before you close your eyes to begin your meditation, take a look behind you at the upper back corners (this location is important, and I'll say why later) of the space where you are sitting. Then turn back around, close your eyes and relax.

Technique

- Ground and center yourself.

- Be aware of your energy in the center of your head. Breathe and relax, and move your attention to just above your head. Feel what that feels like, notice if it's familiar, or new.

- Come back into the center of your head and notice what it's like to come back. Breathe.

- Now move your awareness to one of the upper back corners of the room that you just looked at. Simply be there and experience what it's like to have a little space from your body. Give your body a little space from the intensity of you, to take a moment for yourself; get in touch with your energy and enthusiasm, your energy as spirit.

- Notice what it's like up there. Have whatever your experience is; let it be. Then gently come back down toward your body. Stop just above your head, be still and know yourself; say hello to yourself as spirit internally, and say hello to your body. Gently move back into the center of your head, and take a nice deep breath.

- Release energy down your grounding and feel what it feels like to be back in your body; notice the shift. It may be dramatic or subtle; it may change over time. Let yourself be aware of what it's like right now.

- Once again move your energy, your attention, your focus from the center of your head and directly up to one of the upper back corners behind you. Hang out there and experience yourself; allow a little space from your current projects and relationships and desires. Get perspective from allowing a little breath in between you and all that you are doing in your body this lifetime. Let yourself be renewed by your own energy as spirit.

- When you are ready come back down, gently come into the center of your head and rest there.

- Repeat this technique at least five times.

- Now practice simply going from the center of your head into the corner of the room and back again several more times as quickly as is comfortable for you, just to experience how effortless it can become.

- The point of this quick repetition is to facilitate releasing any effort that can arise from the analytical part of your mind trying to understand and figure out what the heck you are doing. The more you do it, the easier it becomes.

- This technique is great to use when you need a little break from all that you are doing. It is also helpful when you are processing a lot of intense emotion or pain, or want to get in touch with a new level of your own creativity.

Important Tips for this Exercise

- ✧ Always ground and center first. It will allow you to be present in your energy, allowing your body to feel comfortable and safe, plus it gives you a baseline to start from before venturing out.

- ✧ For this particular technique, *always* go to the upper back corner of the room. This is important because if you move your attention behind your body it will perceive you differently than if you go up and in front of it. Going up and in front of your body before it is ready can create tension or anxiety; your body might think, "Hey! I am so not ready to die right now. What the heck are you doing? Come right back here!" If your body is not used to the idea yet that you can move independently from it, there is no reason to stress it out needlessly! Going behind yourself will allow more relaxation and avoid unnecessary struggle for you and your body. We want your body to feel safe and comfortable. This is also why you looked at the corners before you started; this way your body knows where you are going.

- ✧ Let go of the idea that this practice has to look or feel a certain way. Let it be whatever it is, whether subtle or profound. Let it be about the experience you are having, not what you think you should be having. You don't have to see anything; if you do, wonderful, but that's not the point. I have had students who found no visual aspects to this experience at all. This technique is more about experiencing yourself as spirit separate from the body, however that occurs for you in the moment.

Another Added Benefit

Many people have said to me that when they try to meditate, they immediately fall asleep. That is an example of your body being the one who chooses where your energy is and how it is going to move. It is the "executive" of the show. Sleep is another time when you as spirit are out of the body (see Chapter 19, on dreams). I invite you to use the corner of the room technique to start to take that decision-making power back from your body and make it a partnership, one where you as spirit are senior. One benefit in taking charge of where you are in relation to your body is that you get to decide when you are there or not. Sleep can come easily when you want it, rather than being an effort or occurring at inopportune times.

Having said that, I want to add that there are *definitely* times when you will get the signal that you just must sleep, and it *is* absolutely the right thing to do even though it isn't bedtime. Listen to your intuition, and if it feels right then allow yourself to lie down and "leave" for a few minutes. *In other words, take a short nap.* There are times when the only way to process energy is to do it out of the body. That is perfectly fine. Remember it isn't about which is good or bad, it is about being at choice and using both being in and out of your body in your spiritual unfoldment.

Corner of the room is a simple technique that can help you get perspective on a problem. It can also be a way to reconnect with your enthusiasm and joy and to remember who you are as spirit. You are not your body. You are not your relationship or your job or your family or your creations or your talents, you are spirit. You are that which funds all that you do, all that you create. You are one with the All That Is. Your creations are wonderful and important, but they are not who you are; they do not define you, either good or bad. Going to the corner of the room can help you to remember this. When you know that you are not your problems or your challenges, or even your successes, there is a great sense of freedom and wonder. You are a spiritual being, expressing though physical reality, but not bound by it. You are eternal. You are light.

CHAPTER 9

Gold Energy vs. White Light

The first time I can remember hearing about white light, I was in my mid-teens, driving with one of my girlfriends around a park in Tacoma, Washington, in her VW bug. She was telling me that if I ever need to be protected I could just imagine myself surrounded by white light. I took it in without question, given she was a year older than I. When I imagined it, I saw it in my mind as this light that was the "color" white—like white plastic, etched glass or a white force field. I liked the idea of white light, and I heard many people mention it in the years that followed.

The first time I heard about gold energy I was 19; my friend and teacher at the time mentioned it as a side topic when he was explaining how to work with energy in a particularly intense environment. He said to surround myself with gold. I countered that I already knew about white light as a protection. He went on to say that he preferred gold, that it was a very powerful energy and would raise my vibration while at the same time keep me from harm. He also mentioned that it was a kind of angelic energy and the people I would be dealing with would be very surprised to find me using it since it was from a more advanced place than they would expect me to be in at the time. I again took it in without question and was very determined to keep my energy at "gold" for the duration of the experience. I am sure that I spent a lot more effort than I really needed to do it, but it was still really effective and made a lasting impression on me.

The tradition that I later spent a number of years in and from which I draw a lot of my techniques was also based around using a gold vibration of energy. It was the energy we used for healing; it was what we cleared physical spaces with, the energy we filled ourselves with when we meditated. I learned a lot about it during that time, and I still use it as a primary vibration in my own practice.

Over the years, people have become so much more aware of energy and how to work with it consciously. I love that! I still often hear from people when they first begin to work with energy and want to protect themselves or do healing, that you should "fill yourself up with white light." I recognize that there are a lot of different ways to work, and they are all ultimately valid. However, I wanted to put some of my opinions about working with white light versus gold energy into print so that more people can make informed choices and understand some of the energetic mechanics of how vibrations work. I am not going to say that it is wrong to work with white light, and in fact I have encountered some Native American traditions in which it works very well. I will say, though, that I have seen white light *as it is often used* not be particularly useful or helpful for your energy system.

To give some background, I want to go into the idea of energy for a moment. We are all energy; in fact everything is energy in some form. It is all a dance of vibration. The table my computer is sitting on is energy, the ideas coming out of my mind are energy, the light coming out of the monitor is energy and the letters that seem like they are on a page on the screen are also energy. Our bodies are energy, as well as our thoughts and feelings.

We are beings of energy. The tricky thing with spirit is that we normally have a vibration that is so fast that it can be invisible to the human eye. How we experience reality has to do, in part, with how all these vibrations interact. Since this is a planet of dichotomies, it is easy to get into the idea of good and bad when thinking about vibrations, and there are certainly energies that I prefer over others. For our purposes, though, it is more accurate to think of faster and slower vibrations, or of vibrations that work in harmony with our evolution, or impede the flow.

To come more fully into this reality and into our physical bodies, we have to raise the vibration of the body to some degree so that it is easier for our spiritual essence to be more conscious within the physical. This isn't because the body is some lower thing that is less than spirit. All things are really one anyway, so it wouldn't make sense to say that at all. I am reminded of the quote by Paramahansa Yogananda;

"As water by cooling and condensation becomes ice, so thought by condensation assumes physical form. Everything in the universe is thought in material form."

Physical matter is, just by its nature, a slower/longer vibration, which is one of the reasons we can see it (that along with an agreed-upon belief system that creates the appearance of matter, but I digress). More importantly, most of us have spent much of our current and even past lifetimes filling our physical forms with a lot of unwanted ideas, thoughts, concepts and energy. We have learned a lot of things that go against our essential nature, and therefore slow the vibration of the body down from what it could be naturally. One of the aspects of what is referred to as "enlightenment" is simply a process of releasing the things which burden us and slow our energy down. We all come from light. As we become less "dense" we experience more of what we already are, and become "enlightened."

So this brings me back to vibration. Colors have vibration. We can consciously use colors in our process of healing, working with magic and increasing or raising consciousness. Energy vibration can be interpreted as color internally, just as the visible spectrum of light is seen by our eyes and interpreted as color by our brains. That is what clairvoyant readers do when they see the colors of your aura. They are interpreting the vibration and bringing it into a usable form. I was taught that there are really no bad or good aura colors, that what one wants to look for is clarity in the color and movement in the energy. We use different colors for different things, and all vibrations have a place in the spectrum.

The two vibrations I want to now look at are gold and white. Why do so many people equate what is thought of as "white light" as being the best thing to use, the great protective all-encompassing ideal to strive for? It occurs in many New Age texts, and some religious ideologies, including paganism. I don't know how many times I have heard someone say that he or she isn't a "bad" witch but a "white" witch (which includes the idea that *energy* itself can somehow be good or bad, as opposed to how one uses it being the deciding factor). But it is understandable in some ways. In this culture, we have a distinct connection with white equals good. The good guys wear the white hats; the bad guys are often in black. We have grown up with this idea. This is not true universally; in some cultures white equals death, and is not something that you aspire to. But in this culture, if you are filling yourself up with "white" then you must be good somehow. Well, first of all you *are* good; everything is essentially at its core good, and there is nothing that can change that, even if we stray off the experience of that Truth in any given life. So using white isn't going to make you any more spiritual then using blue or purple. All vibrations come from the same source. However, using white will affect your experience.

The problem, as I see it, with using white light in this reality is that the vibration has been altered by our concepts of color. When we think of 'white" we think of the color of paper or the color of milk or of Elmer's glue. And that is essentially the issue. When you take an energy, such as the light of spirit, the full spectrum of all creation and try to cram it into the slower vibration of physical reality you get something that looks a whole lot like white glue, and acts a lot like it as well. White light, as it is often used, is a very sticky, thick and slow-moving energy. It will certainly protect, because it allows no movement either in or out. But vibration doesn't "like" to be still; it's all about movement and flow.

White energy can stick things into your energy like glue. Often when people are in fear, they will have a lot of white energy in their aura. Or if someone is afraid for them or of them, it will sometimes turn into a white energy. It is very difficult to see through, so your spiritual sight is blocked. It is also hard to know how you feel or what is happening to your physical body for that same reason. It's like being in a white-out.

So you might ask why anyone would use it and why so many people like it. I can think of two possible reasons: one is that perhaps there are people who truly do not want to feel what their body is feeling, or want so much to be "spiritual" that they would like to just forget all about their physical form. It might be useful for that. Another is that the intention is to experience spiritual light or the light of the Divine, but there is some confusion about how to go about it. I really think the problem lies with the way we think about and therefore create the experience of it. In my experience, it was that I was simply thinking about it incorrectly.

The real trick with white energy is how you visualize it. White light, when you move away from the idea of milk and paper, is actually the full spectrum of color. It includes *all* color. It is the white light from our grade-school science class. It is the light that we *do not see as a color* as it passes through something like a prism, and breaks into the spectrum. Actual white light is what illuminates. It is bright but clear! I tell people in my practice that when they want to work with white light, to visualize it as clear light. That way it is an entirely different experience, and does not impede but rather enhances the flow of energy.

When you use it this way, it is nothing like glue. However, it is a fast enough vibration that it is not always the first thing you want to work with starting out, if you want to create harmony between body and spirit. Kind of like trying to step on a treadmill that is already going ten miles an hour when you are starting from zero, it can be quite a shock, and it's easy to trip and find yourself landing firmly on your behind.

Harmony is one of the things that we are here learning about, which is why I teach people to use gold. I also use it myself a great deal. Gold cosmic energy works in harmony with both physical and spiritual realities. It is not related to "good" or "bad" and can help us to find neutrality within our intense experiences on planet Earth, so that we can remember we are spirit and we are not what we are currently creating, no matter what that experience looks like in the moment.

It is also a high vibration that will increase the vibration of the body, making it easier to come into harmony with it as spirit, yet it is not stressful for the body. It is a vibration that is wonderful for healing since it is soothing, and also neutralizes non-beneficial energy. It is fabulous as a way of clearing space and then owning that cleared space, because much of the energy you might want to clear cannot stay at the level that gold vibrates at.

I was taught that gold energy is also referred to as Christ force energy. If the word "Christ" pushes your buttons, please know that I am not saying it is Jesus force energy and therefore only Christian, although it certainly is a vibration that is associated with the man Jesus. But that is because he was an example of the Christ principle in action. So was Buddha, and many other avatars; plus gold energy is associated with various gods and goddesses. Christ, as I have to remind myself, is a title and not a last name.

Christ means anointed in Greek. In the case of Sanskrit, it is a possible derivative from the term *Krishna* and means "all attractive" and is a term for God. As I understand it, the Christ force is the energy of the spiritual seed within everyone; it is the God/Goddess self, the Awakened One. Using this energy puts us in contact with this inner essence of ourselves and helps us to realize it on this physical plane.

The bottom line, though, is that it works. Using gold as a cleansing and healing energy can shift your perspective, heal old wounds, help clarify situations and generally help to get you in touch with your own spiritual perspective on life. It will also assist you to gently release from your body old burdens and open to your own path.

I work with many different vibrations, so gold is not the only one that I use by a long shot. But it is the one that sets the foundation of the work that I do. I practice various color meditations, and I allow them each to be a teacher to me. Gold, however, is one of my favorites. It is simple, amazingly powerful and very accessible.

I invite you to play with this vibration. Experience it. If you aren't familiar with using energy consciously in your body, then give yourself some time to acclimate. Start with it a little at a time, 10 to 20 minutes, and as you get used to it, you can begin to allow it to flow whenever. As you get comfortable with it, experiment with the shade of gold that you are using. Let it be clear and not dense. Rather than thinking of it like a gold coin, think of it as that warm golden light that sometimes comes right before sunset, when whatever it touches lights up and glows with more depth and beauty than it did the moment before.

Technique

- Begin by grounding and centering, allowing yourself to relax and breath.

- Create a gold sun over your head. Let that gold vibration begin to fill you up. Let it flow through your body and energy system, soothing and healing you.

- Allow it to wash away any discomfort.

- Let it absorb and neutralize any pain or toxins that may be in your awareness. Let it neutralize the energy of these things.

- Be with that gold energy; connect with it.

- Use it to experience a new perspective on the things in your life. Remember who you are; you are spirit, part of the Divine. Breathe and simply allow yourself to be.

- When you are done, open your eyes, bend forward and touch your hands to the floor, as you relax your neck and release any built-up energy around the head and shoulders into the earth.

Section Two
Techniques for Personal Growth

Lesson in Balance

When we swim we strike a delicate balance
we bridge the gap between air and water
motion helps to keep us afloat
gliding forward or in circles

Some of us keep to the top quite easily
hair not wet, head well above the waves
Then there are those of us who dive deep
swimming long spans without a pause
eyes open we sink down and make this our world

but even so we are forced, in time, to the surface
we cannot take the water into our lungs

It is not how we are made

We travel between two distinct worlds
The air from which we take our breath
And the pressured depths
which slow our movements, but support our forms all around

The light bends differently here
From above we can see our goals clearly
and so we dive straight in... sure of our position
Only to find unseen currents pulling at us, and the object we seek
in a position other than we expected

Things change underwater

In time we learn about this, and know how to adjust;
how far forward, how far back, how far down,
we set our goals
but take into account the medium through which we move
less of a fight, more of a dance

I often need to be reminded that I am swimming at all
Sometimes it takes a look from someone else in the water
or I think of a movie I have seen, and it stirs in me something
that speaks of how the air can feel

Gliding on the line between the worlds
I have to remember to breathe
it's minute to minute and there is always the temptation to forget

Because under the water I look up and all I see of the surface
is a moving sheet of diffuse light
the longer I look the denser it seems,
it starts to become a wall

until I catch a movement above me
And I burst up through the illusion, sending waves all around
I see again that I am only swimming

I may be in the water,
the water may be in me to my bones
But I am only swimming
at any moment I may fly

—Erika Ginnis 1989

CHAPTER 10

Letting Go to Have

In this chapter, I am going to address two different subjects. One is an energy that I refer to as "havingness." The other is a technique that is called a "mock-up". These two things go very well together, and I always teach about them in the same session. I am also going to discuss how the act of letting go is essential in order to fully experience and work with these two aspects of spiritual practice.

Havingness is simply the ability to have as one's own, to have physical things, to have spiritual things. To allow yourself to receive the bounty of all that surrounds you. What you can "have," you tend to create for yourself as Spirit. All the things that are present in your life are to some degree an expression of your havingness.

When I was 17 years old, I flew on an airplane to Hawaii. I remember it being cloudy in Seattle when I left (not unusual), and that, as we climbed higher in the plane, we started to go through the cloud cover. Eventually, we broke through all the grayness and were flying above the clouds. The sky was bright blue with brilliant clear sunshine. The clouds below us looked like a billowy carpet. One of the things that I realized while I was on that plane flying in the blue sky with the cloud cover below us (looking like it went on forever), was that the sun didn't go away when it was cloudy, I just couldn't see it because of the clouds.

Okay, fine, this may seem like a really simple idea to you, but to me, at 17, it was a major revelation. I guess without realizing it, I had thought that when it was cloudy and rainy, there wasn't any sun, that it went away somehow. Flying in that plane, I saw that if you rose above the clouds on any day, the sun was always shining, and there was always blue sky.

I was so psyched that I was actually laughing while I was in the plane. My parents just thought I was odd, which is actually pretty true. But I am reminded of that image when I think about havingness, the ability to have.

For a long time, I thought that either you had the ability to have, or you had to go get some somewhere. Maybe I thought there was a havingness store someplace. I can remember many times trying hard to acquire more havingness or prosperity, but havingness is a spiritual ability and so the effort of trying hard didn't do me much good. It was pretty frustrating, sometimes, because I reasoned that if I could just do the right thing or be the right person I would have the experience of having what I wanted. So, if the reverse was true of my life, then it must mean that there was something lacking in me! How annoying!

Many years ago, one of my teachers mentioned to me that I already had the ability to have and that all I needed to do was clear the blocks that were in my way to experiencing my own spiritual ability. I suddenly heard that in a new way. I already had the ability to have. I didn't need to be something else, to be more spirit (whatever that means); I already had the ability. It reminded me of rising above the clouds in the plane.

I believe that this is true of everyone. You already are spirit; you already have the ability to have, to receive, but you may be experiencing blocks to that ability. I think of the blocks like clouds. The love of the Universe is always there, a shining clear light; it doesn't go away, but sometimes there are clouds or blocks in the way, and it makes it hard to experience or receive.

That's where letting go comes in; recognizing the blocks, and starting to let them go, creates movement in the energy. If you find yourself clinging to things, you may find that what you really are putting your energy into is lack, not havingness.

I had the experience a few years ago of feeling incredibly poor, I had no idea where my money was going to come from for rent or food, and I was pretty scared. One day, I was driving along and saw a man by the side of the road with a sign asking for money and food. I only had about three dollars in my pocket, but I had this thought that I wanted to give this guy some money. So that's what I did, and it made me feel so good. I felt like I had something to give. By letting go of that money at that time, I was also letting go of the concept of lack and replacing it with the idea that if I had something to give him, that must mean I had something after all. My monetary situation got much better after that.

By that act of giving up, I started to let go of some of my own blocks to having. I tell this story for a couple of reasons. One is that it is a nice example of these ideas; the other reason is to show that this is an ongoing process. There are layers to things, and we all work on them to some degree throughout our lives. Don't feel bad if you find that you continue to do work on all these techniques and principles.

Sometimes, when I teach people to experience their own energy of havingness, I am surprised by how much resistance it brings up in them. I used to think... well, hmm, why is that? It should be *fun!* But in reality, when you start to get in touch with this ability it can bring up all those things that have blocked it in the past. Many times, the things that block us are ideas that we aren't worthy or deserving. Self-esteem issues come up, or past painful situations. These are all things that can feel unpleasant to deal with but feel fabulous to release!

We may also come across an idea that it isn't "right" for us to have because there are people around us who don't have as much. Or that it is somehow "evil" to have. The way I look at it is that it's hard to redistribute the wealth if you have none to redistribute.

I have also found that when people know that they can have from the abundance of the Universe without hoarding or taking away from someone else, they become much more giving people. I hesitate to judge other people's experiences because I know for myself, that I have had incredibly valuable lessons that came to me through the guise of situations and circumstances that seemed less than ideal.

The good news is that you can rise above your limits to having. You are spirit, and you can let go and release the blocks that prevent you from having and receiving Infinite Love, your clear communication as spirit, a new house, a new job, money, whatever it is that you want to have.

I personally have found that meditation (big surprise), magic, prayer, or some form of energy work that includes turning within and recognizing the incredible abundance of the Universe can really be a healing force. And something else—you can request help, from a friend, an angel, God/dess. You can allow yourself to have assistance in clearing the blocks. All you need to do is ask.

What if you're not even sure what it is that you want to have. Why not ask for clarity in knowing what it is that you want? One of the things I personally believe is that the Universe likes to give; all you have to do is ask and then allow yourself to receive. I also believe that there is an ever-shining light, the light of you as spirit, a spark of the Divine, the light of the God/Goddess, waiting to shine into your life. It's not like small samples of light and joy doled out sparingly, but all those things just waiting to come to you. Ask for what you want, and clear the blocks. Let the clouds move away and see that the sun is always shining and you already have the spiritual ability of havingness.

In the next section, I will outline how to get in touch with this energy and also how to work with something called a "mock-up." A mock-up is simply a way to clearly create what you want.

Technique

- Close your eyes and turn within. Ground and center yourself; begin to create and destroy roses. If you don't know what I mean by this, read through the previous chapters on these topics.

- Think of a time within the last week when you let yourself have something that you wanted. Notice what this felt like. Release energy.

- Now, think of a time within the last week when you didn't let yourself have something you wanted, or you received something and you weren't really able to have it. Notice what this felt like. Create and destroy roses, and release energy down your grounding; let that experience go.

- As you relax and breathe, create a big energy ball of your own unique vibration of havingness above your head. Let this energy flow into your body through the top of your head. Let it fill your body and your aura. Be aware of what this feels like.

- Release any non-permission energy down your grounding. Use your ability to create and destroy roses, and clear any ideas or thoughts that come up for you that would limit your experience of being able to have. Release doubts and fears, anything that says you are somehow unworthy; release your own or other people's concepts that you may have taken on over the course of your life that say you can't have or that receiving has to be painful. Realize that this will be the start of a process; you don't have to do this all at once! Breathe... and relax; know that you are spirit. You are not any of your experiences or problems; you are a spark of Divinity incarnate. Sit with this energy for a while; get acquainted with it.

Mock-ups

- Continue to ground and center and experience your havingness. Think of something that you would like to have for yourself. It can be anything, physical or spiritual, you choose. Create and destroy roses.

- Imagine and create a pink helium balloon out in front of you. Put that thing you want into the balloon. Let the balloon go, watch it float up and away until you can't see it any more. Create and destroy roses for anything that would prevent you from letting the mock-up go, or from having the thing you want once you get it. Ground and breathe.

You can create a mock-up for anything you wish. There are no limits to how many mock-ups you can create. Just like with any magic/energy work I suggest you make mock-ups for things for yourself personally so that you don't invade someone else's reality. For example, it will work much better to send up a mock-up for "a romantic relationship that works really well for me and that I am happy with" than to send up one for "a romantic relationship with John/Jane Doe over there at the next table, whom I have never met". For any of you who have done magic/prayer of the second type, you know that, even if you get what you asked for, it usually ends up not being what you really wanted.

Please be aware that you will get what you wish for, whether in this life or the next. Okay, consider yourself warned! You can always create and destroy roses for old mock-ups that you no longer want. This helps avoid the "Oh, great, now I have ten toasters even though I already found the one I want" syndrome.

Some things to remember about mock-ups:

- ✧ Know what you want (even if what you want is to *know* what you want).
- ✧ They have to be possible in this reality (a mock-up for being able to fly is fine, but include the plane).
- ✧ You need some kind of faith or belief (not a huge amount, just start where you are and it will grow). You can do a mock-up for more belief if you like.
- ✧ You need to be ready to *let the mock-up go*. If you hold on to it and never let it go, it can't return to you. Ever had the experience of wanting something so bad you

could taste it? Of never getting it, and then when you finally don't care anymore, you get ten of whatever it was (the toaster thing again)?

- You need to be able to *have/receive* the mock-up once it comes to you. If you can't let yourself have it, you will either only get it for a little while, or you won't be able to see the thing when it is staring you in the face. You might laugh at this, but I see it happen all the time.

- Have fun, let it be like play. If you add amusement everything will be much easier and more enjoyable.

- Work with your havingness energy, add it to your daily meditations. It really makes a big difference. Enjoy your creativity. Creating a notebook to record your mock-ups and when you receive them can be a validating exercise. You are spirit; you can begin to consciously create the life you would like. It may take time and patience, but I personally think it is completely worth it.

CHAPTER 11

Dealing with Growth Periods

One idea I have found essential when working with personal growth, especially when spiritual changes are being made, is that of a "growth period." Very simply put, a growth period is the time it takes your physical body to process and adjust to the changes you make as spirit.

Have you ever taken a class in some kind of personal development or spiritual work, and felt like you were riding an amazing high, only to find yourself a week or two later getting sick or wanting to hide from the world? Or perhaps you made a lot of changes in your life and were really excited, and then a little while later all you want to do is lie on your couch and watch TV? No, you were not being a slacker! These are examples of growth periods.

The way it works is relatively simple. First of all, you make some kind of change or work on something as spirit. This happens very quickly, since spirit isn't bound by time and space.

Great, no problem, you can make all these changes and wheeeee! Right? Well, only partially. You are spirit; you can change in an instant. However, *you have a body,* and that body has to operate in time and space. So what happens next is that your body needs to integrate what you have changed. It needs time to process the new energy.

While you are in this process, it can feel a little odd. I think of it sometimes like a plant getting a new leaf. When the leaf is just beginning to unfold, it is a lighter green and is a lot more tender, more easily bruised. It hasn't developed the more waxy finish that the other leaves have.

This is analogous to how we can feel when we are in a state of flux. Over time, the leaf grows out and unfolds and becomes just like the others, and the plant is that much larger. This is the process by which growth occurs. We are not so very different from plants. We don't normally sprout leaves, but our changes are just as real and every bit as observable if you know how to look.

Events like holidays, birthdays, anniversaries or any other cyclic revisiting can prompt an awareness of our growth periods, or create growth periods. Even when you are very solid in your path, have been meditating every day and are all caught up on your reading — like we all are, right? — it is hard to dismiss all that these events bring up in us. All our associated childhood experiences, good or bad, are there with us. All the hopes and dreams, realized or not, come crowding back to us. We get together with family members, and sometimes it seems like we become someone we once were, or never were but thought we were supposed to be.

That may be why it has been said that a prophet is not without honor, except in his or her own house. When the prophets were home, they may have been too busy dealing with their pasts and family issues, the cyclic and therefore mortal aspects of themselves, to put themselves forward as prophets. I recently spoke with a woman who was surprised that she had stuff come up around her birthday. Hello! Cycles, growth periods — we all have them.

Learning new spiritual techniques also creates periods of accelerated growth, so if you have been reading this book and practicing these techniques you may experience some kind of growth period. I have personally found meditation and spiritual study to be a great opportunity for growth and change. The way I look at it is, "If my stuff is going to be up and strewn all around me anyway, I might as well take this opportunity to work on some of it!"

The effects of these periods of accelerated growth may show up in a number of ways. You may want to sleep much more than usual or not need as much sleep as you are used to. You may want to have a lot of sex or want to go out dancing more often, or maybe want to hibernate at home all of a sudden. Maybe you want to eat a lot of chocolate, or you may catch a cold, or just feel generally unsettled. It may also be that you feel better than you ever have and you feel like the whole world is opening up to you.

Growth periods are not always bad or uncomfortable, although those are the ones we often recognize. It's just as likely that a growth period is a feeling of expansion, an amazing experience of greater good. You may be doing things differently than you have ever done them before, and *they work better!* A growth period can show up as mind-blowing connection with a loved one, not just the desire to hide under a rock. It is all change. It still requires adjustment. If you are used to being alone and misunderstood, and all of a sudden you find yourself in relationship with someone who understands and appreciates you, you are going to have to adjust, and that will take time! The time it takes is the growth period.

You may have heard the term "dark night of the soul." While that can mean many things to many people, it is certainly an apt phrase for some kinds of growth periods. Sometimes when you are in the middle of a growth period, light seems like a distant memory. I want to share with you an analogy that has been helpful to me.

If you are walking through a dark tunnel (analogous to your spiritual journey, or even one portion of that journey), at first you are surrounded by light. You are at the beginning; you can see where you are going; you know that you are entering a tunnel on purpose and that it will have an end to it. Some time later (read, as you are going into your growth period), you notice it is getting darker, but you feel okay about that since you can still see from the light behind you, coming from where you have started.

At *some time* in your journey, you are going to be at the midpoint. At that midpoint, if it is a large enough tunnel, you are going to be in pitch black. You won't be able to see the light where you came from, and the light you are going toward won't be visible yet (note that it isn't gone; it just isn't visible at the moment). I have tested this out in a real tunnel, and sure enough it got really, really dark, I couldn't see anything. All I could hear was the dripping of water from the ceiling and my own footsteps. I got very uncomfortable — one might say *scared*, even.

The trick, whether you are in a tunnel or in a huge growth period, is to remember to *keep moving!* If you have the desire to turn around and run back (which you are always free to do), remember you will still have *exactly the same amount of distance to travel*, but you will arrive back where you started. If, however, you keep moving forward (a former teacher of mine would say, "crawl... drag yourself along, it doesn't matter how fast you go, just don't stop") in the direction that you headed out, then eventually you will see a teeny-tiny point of light, and if you keep going that light will grow larger. Eventually, you will be able to see all around you, and you will arrive at your intended destination.

"So why all this talk about tunnels?" you ask. Simple, it is because we do this all the time, and especially when we are starting something new. We begin, we hit a growth period, and then we want to quit, because we get scared. We ask for change, and when we get it we are unhappy because things are different!

What is important, especially when the process feels challenging, is to remember this is a normal, natural and necessary part of learning and growing. Many of us like to try to skip this part, or try to ignore it. We may feel more fragile at this time and want to protect ourselves by denying our changes. Unfortunately, one of the things that denial can do is to prolong the process. If you acknowledge your growth period, you can then begin to communicate with your body about what's happening and what your body needs. Communication will make it all go more smoothly.

Sometimes all it takes is that conscious recognition that you are indeed in a growth period. It can make it all make more sense. Another thing to remember is that growth periods are cyclic... they have a beginning, a middle and an end! They don't go on forever; you will adjust to the changes, and you will have grown. Remember the old adage: "This too shall pass".

As long as you are in a body, you will have growth periods; it's part of the package. If you are into growing spiritually, well, guess what, you will go out of your way to have growth periods! I find that meditation really helps to keep everything flowing. It may be that the time that you want to meditate the least is when you need it the most. Becoming aware of your own growth is a fabulous time to commit to meditating daily.

One of the techniques that I suggest people use for getting a handle on where they are in their growth is as follows: Find a quiet place where you won't be disturbed for a few minutes. (Sure, you say, with all my family and pets wanting my attention, how will this happen? If all else fails, go into the bathroom, lock the door and say you're taking a bath.) Take a few minutes to ground and center.

Let yourself become aware of what your current growth period is; let the information flow to you from your stillness. Ask yourself the question: "What are the spiritual changes I have recently made, and how am I responding to them?" Let the answers flow. Maybe you have been feeling odd and unsettled and not wanted to look at it, so have been on the run as much as possible to avoid it all. Take this opportunity to stop running and simply look at what's happening and why, and give yourself permission to not take it all so seriously. Laugh a little at the huge growth period you are in (if this is the case). Even if the issue that you are working on is serious, treating it with just a little amusement can help the energy move and change more easily.

The next exercise can give you more insight into what you are working on and can also act as a wonderful way to get in touch with your own changes.

✧ Take two sheets of paper and a pen. On the first sheet, start the heading of a letter that says "Dear Spirit..." and at the end of the sheet of paper write "... love, Body." Next, take the other sheet of paper and at the top write "Dear Body...." and at the end of the paper write "...love, Spirit."

- ✧ If you haven't already guessed, you are going to write two letters. Let your mind relax and let your body have a voice; let it talk to you and let you know what's up, what it feels, what it needs. Write it down in the first letter. This is your body communicating to you, the spiritual being. Don't judge what you write, just write. It may say things like, "Dear Spirit, you haven't been paying any attention to me. I need more exercise; I need more sleep; please buy me some flowers." Or perhaps, "I am trying as best as I can, but I don't know what we are doing or where we are going, so I am afraid; please let me know what's going on." Or even, "I am starting to get a cold; please drink a lot of water so I won't be sick for my vacation/wedding/new job."

- ✧ Whatever the communication, the letter is a valuable tool for staying in touch with the wisdom of the body and for knowing how your body actually feels in this often hectic life. Now, realize you don't have to do everything the body asks for. It may say, "I want to go escape to Hawaii from September until February," but what you as spirit may decide to do is go spend 10 minutes tanning and take a walk in a conservatory of tropical plants. What you may find is that the very act of being listened to is enough to totally change how your body feels.

- ✧ Next up is the second letter. This is a letter from you as spirit to your body. Take a minute and breathe and relax. Get in touch with yourself and your own inner voice. I highly recommend meditating as part of writing both these letters if it is at all possible. This is the letter that begins, "Dear Body...." You may be surprised at what you write. Let go of your expectations as you write and let it flow. It may sound like, "Dear Body, I love you, but I am not always good at communicating, but I am working on changing that.

> I want to work on prosperity and ease, and so I have stimulated all the memories from our childhood so I can put them to rest. Sorry I didn't mention this to you before I started." Or, "I am really proud of the way you didn't get enough sleep for a few days so that I could create that wonderful art project I have wanted to do. I am going to make sure there is time now to relax and enjoy the next week."

Your letter may also sound totally different than these examples, which is the point. It is your own voice as spirit communicating into this physical reality to your amazing body so that you can begin to work in harmony with each other. It is all part of the same thing, but it has different aspects and different voices, which are each valid and valuable. I often say that one of our most important relationships, one that colors all our others, is the one we have as spirit with our body. If we can begin to harmonize that one, the others are much more likely to be successful.

Becoming aware of the changes and harmonizing with them is important not only for us personally, but for ourselves as humans in the larger sense, and also our planet (which is our larger body). We are all in a huge growth period right now. There are big shifts and changes taking place. Some of them are spiritual (such as that feeling that life is happening faster than it used to... no, it isn't your imagination, it's true we are raising our collective vibration).

Some of them occur as physical changes, such as tsunamis, climate shifts and earthquakes. In the case of the 2004 Indonesian earthquake that caused the tsunami, we literally shaved off some small (not noticeable but still measurable) amount of time off our actual day, 2.68 microseconds. (For more information, see the website http://www.jpl.nasa.gov/news/news.cfm?release=2005-009.)

These physical changes can really get our attention, and we can see very clearly that once they take place we need to process and adjust to them. What's equally true is that there are energy shifts happening within each and every one of us. The phenomenon is happening everywhere. I sometimes think of it like a giant birthing, with ourselves and our planet as being both the mother and the child. We are emerging into our next stage of being. This has been happening for a long time, in a subtle way, but now the shifts are more pronounced and harder to ignore. There are a lot of opportunities for growth and change.

I hope now that you have some tools to use during this time of change and renewal, and you can let yourself enjoy what comes to you and be able to learn from it. If nothing else, you can know what is going on when you want nothing better than to stay in bed and eat chocolate or watch that movie marathon from beginning to end. It is just a growth period! Next week, most likely, you'll be planning what new plants you want to add to your garden, enjoying your new way of seeing the world or beginning that new class you wanted to take.

I will end with another saying I heard a lot when I was a student: "Running your energy will get you into a growth period, and running your energy will also get you out!" Meditate, meditate, meditate. It puts everything into perspective.

CHAPTER 12

Dealing with the Shadow Things in Life

We live in a reality of dichotomies. Things are split into their opposites or complements in physical reality. Good/bad, light/dark, inner/outer: the list isn't hard to come up with. I do personally believe that who we are in capital "R" Reality is energy. I believe that we are spirit, and spirit can be perceived as Light. When I say Light (again with a capital "L"), I don't mean just light that we think of in our dichotomy of light/dark, good/bad, right/wrong—since that is usually a judgment call, mostly made of our perspective at present, which is by its nature limited and changeable—but the Light that is all things and encompasses, balances and completes all dichotomies.

However, we are here incarnating into the physical plane (mundane reality), and to do this we each have a body. We find ourselves involved in and surrounded by the world of opposites. We are in a process or a game of learning, and this world of opposites is one of the "playing fields" that we are currently using. I am of the opinion that we are here uncovering our true nature, and that this is a process of "becoming" who we actually are. In this process, we come across our shadow aspects. These can actually be very powerful allies if we look them right in the eye and make peace with them. They can also be the driving force in our lives if we deny them or avoid them entirely.

I have been doing psychic readings, healing and teaching people how to work with their energy since the early 1980s. In that time, I have had numerous opportunities to see in someone something that would be considered "shadow." I have also had the opportunity to see or experience "shadow" within myself. In fact, one of the things that I run into a lot with people who find out that I read auras, is that they are immediately curious—"What color is my aura?"—and also afraid—"Oh, no, maybe you'll see something really bad." I think it's that fear that keeps us from exploring our inner nature much of the time.

In some ways, our fears are unfounded; we, as spirit, are always greater than that we fear. But there is also the reality that we all have shadow within us. What you can't get around when you are either learning to work with energy or are reading someone is, "When you turn on the light, you're going to start to see." That means you'll see the shadow as well as the light. If you fear and avoid the shadow within you then you might tend to project that onto others—" I am good…they are bad!"—or you might find yourself afraid to use your own power.

So how, you might ask, do I tell people that they are being completely run by their anger and it's destroying their lives, or that there are seemingly invasive energy beings right in their space actively draining their energy? These instances of shadow have occurred at different times in my work. The answer is: very mindfully, and I hope in a way that they can hear me.

Otherwise, I might as well keep still. I have come up with a list of a few things that I have learned over the years that have assisted me in communicating with people about shadow stuff. It is also very good to use for your own growth, since that is the real point of all this, in my opinion.

Truth

Truth without love can be a hammer. I didn't learn this one until I was in my mid 30s, but I am sure many people in my life were relieved once I did! I find it incredibly important, and it's one of the reasons that it continues to be important to work on yourself. It is really easy just to see something and tell it to someone without any compassion, understanding or love. This helps about as much as hitting them over the head with a hammer; it also feels about the same. If you can come from a place of understanding and truly love the truth of who they are on some level, even if they are dealing with some very difficult things, then you stand a chance of communicating in a way that they might actually hear.

This doesn't mean being "nice," or even presuppose that you have to "like" the person; it also doesn't mean that you will even change what you would say. It just means that you continue to do the work necessary to come from a place of love even in the midst of conflict, and that you are speaking from a desire to communicate the love behind the truth rather than just the "satisfaction" of telling someone what's wrong with them. This is also just as important to do within ourselves as it is for other people.

Neutrality

Neutrality and amusement help with telling someone about their shadow side. One of the things that was important in my training as a reader, and that I also teach people when they work with me, is a technique called neutrality. It simply means operating from a place of non-judgment (not labeling the thing as right or wrong, good or bad). It means seeing what is, not what you "want" to see or what the other person "wants" you to see. It can be incredibly healing for someone when you actually see them, see what's up, speak about it and not judge them for it. It can be extremely powerful in your own personal work as well.

Something else that goes hand in hand with that is amusement. Sometimes, if you can add some lightness into your energy or voice it can really help when you are dealing with "serious" issues. This doesn't mean that you have to joke about everything; sometimes that just isn't helpful. But if you can keep you own energy up out of the morass, then the other person has a much better chance of being able to hear what you have to say.

Perspective

In addition—remember to keep your perspective. If you find when reading one of your past lives that you were someone that spent the entire life cutting off everyone's heads, it is important to keep the perspective that you had something to learn from the experience. Perhaps in that life you needed to be right where you were. This is a challenge, especially when we see things in ourselves that we don't agree with in this life. It's also important to keep perspective when we look at our own past in this life and want to learn from things which we consider our shadow.

Attention

It's important to know what your "stuff" is, but equally important to put your attention on where you want to go. What you put your attention on increases. We probably know this as energy and magic workers. Right? Right! It applies in other areas as well. There is a seductive quality about looking at our inner darkness. We can unwittingly create more of the same if we spend all of our time putting our energy or focus on "what's wrong with us."

Bringing things to our conscious awareness can be a step in healing them, and doing the work necessary to change things can be another step. Making peace with shadow can mean acknowledging it and accepting it as part of the experience of being human. Dwelling on it endlessly will only bring more of the same.

Hearing

People have to be ready to hear what you have to say on some level. I have found this important in doing reading or teaching work. If people aren't ready to hear what you have to say, it won't really matter how you say it; they simply won't hear you. As a reader, I see a lot of things. I simply don't say all of them. That is something that, even though I was taught it in my training as a reader, I didn't really get until much later. If you give someone too much information, they will start throwing it back at you. If you can give enough so that they can hear it, the rest will follow in its own time.

Current Perception

Many things that we perceive as shadow are simply things that served us in the past that are no longer current in our present situation. This is true in past-life situations as well as our current life history. Many of us came from backgrounds in which we needed to develop certain skills just to deal with the environment, whether that is physical, emotional or spiritual.

They were our keys to survival and therefore were very important to our well-being. The trick is to see that some of those very things that kept us alive in the past may be keeping us from living fully in the present. They got us to where we are today, but are now perhaps actually hindering us.

Having outlived their usefulness, they can cause damage to our lives if we don't discard them. We may experience them as a part of shadow. The bracelet that you had as a child, with your name, address and phone number on it, was quite useful and important at that time. If you had never taken it off, it would probably have become pretty uncomfortable or even damaging at some point.

Forgiveness

Judgment can actually get us stuck in the behavior or energy; forgiveness lets us release and move on. Forgiveness can help you set it aside and get on with what you are doing. When we get into judgment about something, it is like psychic glue that sticks us to whatever we are judging. The Universe has a sense of humor in all this, because the bad news is: Eventually we will start to emulate the very thing we were judging.

So it is in our own best interest to forgive ourselves or others, since it then frees us to move on. This doesn't mean staying involved with things that don't work for us. It does mean releasing the judgment (or energy) about them and about ourselves for what our involvement is or has been so that we can continue to grow. When we start to see the shadow in our nature and accept it, then we can expand our awareness of who we are and where we are going.

CHAPTER 13

Allowing

This chapter is about allowing. Now, you might ask yourself, "What is that?" For me, it is easier to start with what I have found out that it isn't. It isn't forcing; it isn't looking at something and finding out what is wrong with it and trying to "fix" it so it will be perfect.

It's tough sometimes because much of our culture is focused on fixing, getting it "right," wanting it to be different, "perfect," not owning or acknowledging something until it is finished perfectly. This translates to our own life as well. How often do we simply allow ourselves to be, at any given time?

When we meditate, how much time do we spend trying to "fix" ourselves? I find that it's easy to get caught in that way of thinking. We're constantly trying to fix something in others or in ourselves, looking for that perfect time (in the future, of course) when we will get things right! We think about how happy we'll be "some day", all the things that we'll get accomplished.

I have found that when I am that focused outside myself, I lose touch with me, now. I focus on the great me in the future. I don't allow myself to simply be.

Many years ago, I was taking a drive and I was very focused on what was wrong with me, and I wasn't feeling particularly good about myself. I was at a stoplight, and I looked up from the road and noticed this mountain behind the hills. I was struck with how beautiful the mountain was. As I looked at the mountain, I started to feel better. I realized sitting there that when I saw the beauty of the mountain I wasn't trying to change or fix it. I could simply allow it to be a mountain. I realized how silly it would sound to look at the mountain and say, "Oh, well, it's not really a good mountain. I think it should have more of a peak there, and there's not enough snow over there. Maybe in the future at some point in time, the mountain will be exactly perfect, and then it will be beautiful."

It simply was a mountain. It could change through time, one day snow-covered and the next craggy and bare. It would always be beautiful. If I could simply allow the mountain to be and it was okay, maybe I could allow myself to be too.

I had a similar experience sitting by a river one afternoon in the summer. I noticed three small streams coming off the main river before flowing back downstream. All of these streams were constantly changing, all of them were different; one was so small that you could have easily missed it, but they were all streams and they simply were. They were beautiful, and I felt healed by listening to them and watching them.

As I allowed these streams to simply be, constantly flowing, different every second, but always streams, I began again to get in touch with myself as spirit: changing, experiencing but always me. I may flow over different rocks or "blocks," but the flowing doesn't change the essential me any more than the stream ceases to be a stream just because it is flowing over a different set of rocks one day to the next.

I love being in nature. I have a great affinity with Mother Earth; she is so gracious and powerful and loving and abundant. The mountains and the streams, the flowers and the clouds just are; they don't have to do anything to "fix" themselves. They are glorious just in their existence. I believe that if we can begin to see the glory that is in nature and realize that we are a part of and not apart from this infinite expression, we can see that the Mother has already clothed us in beauty. We are spirit, part of the Divine. The question is: Will we allow ourselves to simply be and notice it?

Perhaps one of the things to cultivate is patience. The trees don't bring forth all the fruit at once; it takes time and seasons and growth. One of the essential ingredients for allowing myself to be, is to have patience with myself. I don't judge the river for the ground it hasn't covered yet. It simply flows and creates its own course over time.

As I watch the streams and enjoy them as they are, I can begin to look at myself differently, bringing into my life some of that same "allowing" that lets me accept and enjoy nature. We all have the ability to allow ourselves to see the beauty that we have simply as we are, regardless of the season.

We can let go of meditating in order to "fix" something and allow our meditation time to be one of communication with self and the infinite. We can simply allow energy to flow, and experience it like water without judging it, letting ourselves make the changes we want but allowing ourselves to be where we are in the present. See yourself as spirit, a spark of the Divine, expressing through your sacred body, in the here and now, allowing yourself to be.

Technique

- Sit back and relax and allow yourself to create a grounding cord.

- Allow yourself to breathe and relax and release down your grounding any tension or discomfort that you may be experiencing.

- Allow yourself to center in that place a little above and behind your eyes, the place where you can reside as spirit in your body and be neutral, that place where you can say yes to yourself.

Releasing Blocks to Allowing

- Create out in front of you an image of a rose. Admire it, and then destroy it.

- Create another rose out in front of you, and as you destroy it allow yourself to release any energy that would block you from simply allowing yourself and others to be.

- Is there anything that says if you accept and allow yourself as you are that you will never change? Create a rose and destroy it, and release energy.

- Are you too busy to simply be? Do you need to be better than the *Divine* made you before you can allow yourself and accept yourself? Create and destroy a rose, and release energy.

- Do you need to make sure everyone else is "fixed" first before you can take the time to see your own beauty?

- Take a nice deep breath, and release energy down your grounding.

Experiencing Yourself

- Create a gold sun above your head, and allow the vibrant gold energy to flow into your space and all around you.

- Take a minute and experience the neutrality of this gold energy.

- Allow yourself to communicate with your own higher self. Relax and tune into that connection.

- Say hello to the Infinite Essence of your Heart. Say hello to that of which you are also a part. It may be known by many names, choose whatever works for you (Goddess, God, the Tao, the Great Spirit, Allah, Universal Mind...).

- Let the energy flow to you as bright, crystal clear light. Allow the crystal-clear energy to flow into your body and fill your energy system; communicate with this essence about allowing yourself to simply be.

- Create and destroy a rose. Take a minute to just experience yourself as you are right now, allowing your self to simply be. When you are done, you can bend forward and release energy.

CHAPTER 14

Willingness

During the summer of 2004, I was contemplating my will and the will of the Universe, or flow if you like, and getting to another level of "I don't have to make things happen, and sometimes I can't make them happen even if I want to." This process brought me to the place of saying, "Okay, so what then?"

In answer, I began to have an experience of the power of being willing. The following list of what I call "Willingnesses" came to me in meditation. I have them printed out on nice paper next to my desk so that I will look at them often.

Willingness has been an incredible force for change in my own life. It has opened me up for wonders and gifts that I could not have experienced if I had clung onto my old ideas and limitations, even if my limitations were my ideas of what should be. When I am willing, it creates an opening for the Universe to work. When I let go and allow the larger ideas of the Universe to present themselves, I often find that it is really the best thing for all concerned, that the good is a good large enough for all concerned and that I am truly blessed.

These short lines have made a huge difference in my life, and I wanted to pass them on. Try them out or make up some of your own.

- ✧ I am willing to be guided by my Higher Self.
- ✧ I am willing to be happy.
- ✧ I am willing for my life to work really well.
- ✧ I am willing to be well-compensated for doing work that I love.
- ✧ I am willing to be financially abundant and make more than enough money to be financially secure and able to give and share and have fun.
- ✧ I am willing for sex to be wonderful and fun.
- ✧ I am willing to be happy, satisfied and fulfilled in my romantic relationships.
- ✧ I am willing to have my life lessons be gentle and graceful.
- ✧ I am willing to enjoy greater and greater levels of positive energy with positive results for myself and others.
- ✧ I am willing for my body to be strong, healthy and flexible and to feel fabulous.

- ✧ I am willing for my mind to become sharper and quicker with age.

- ✧ I am willing to be the Me I was meant to be.

CHAPTER 15

Forgiveness

Forgiveness is an energy, just as all things are energy. Forgiveness is an energy that allows you to release and let go. It is a spiritual ability. What do you think about when you hear the word "forgiveness"? Is it something that only God can do? Well, you are spirit, a bright spark of the Divine Essence, a child of the Goddess, and you have the spiritual ability to forgive.

Forgiveness has to do with letting go, releasing something you no longer want, are completed with. Forgiveness has a lot to do with non-judgment. When you judge, you tend to hang on to whatever it is. Forgiveness allows you to let go of the clenched fists so you can move on without taking unwanted things with you.

As you release judgment about yourself and your creations, about other people and where they are at, you can begin to forgive yourself and others. In so doing, you free yourself from unwanted energy. Forgiveness doesn't have to do with judging something good or bad; it's simply letting go.

Now, sometimes it might seem easier to say to yourself: "Well, I will wait until this is resolved" or "I will forgive this person or event as soon as this or that happens." But what the reality is, in my opinion; either you have forgiven someone or you haven't; you have either allowed yourself to let go or you haven't. Now, I know for myself I always thought of forgiveness as something I would be doing *for* someone else, and so it was difficult for me to imagine forgiving someone when I felt they had wronged me in some way. But when we hang onto, or blame, or judge someone else, then essentially we are holding on to the energy, and it can keep us from experiencing our own unique vibration as freely as we might wish to. It can create tension, anxiety and discomfort. Forgiveness allows motion and healing. So when you are forgiving someone, you are actually *healing yourself* by allowing a cleansing and releasing.

I will relate a story that I heard a long time ago; you may have heard some version of it at some point. A long time ago, there were two men walking along a path in the woods. They were monks of an eastern order, an older man and a younger man, and as such they were not supposed to have any contact with women. As they were walking, they came upon a flowing river, and at the edge of the river was a young woman who had no way to get across. The two monks stopped at the river, and the woman asked them if they would please assist her across the river. The younger monk turned his head so as not to look at her and waded across the river, while the older one picked the woman up and carried her across to the other side, where he set her down again on the river bank and proceeded on his way.

Now the two men walked along in silence, the younger monk the whole while seething inside with indignation, but not saying anything. Some time passed, and finally he could contain himself no longer and burst out "I can't stand it! You're an elder monk. How could you carry that woman across the river?" And the older monk smiled, turned and said, "A half-hour ago, I set the woman down on the bank of the river. You, however, are still carrying her."

I always remembered that story, and I thought of it when I wrote this chapter. How often in our lives do we carry things with us, long after the fact? How many burdens are we still carrying because we judge them? This applies not only to forgiving others, but to forgiving ourselves as well.

I believe that forgiveness is its own reward. It frees up energy and creativity; it allows us to move on. Have you ever noticed that when you finally let something go, you are free to let go of the pattern completely?

As you allow forgiveness, you allow motion. Now the big question is: Can we allow this same information when it comes to ourselves? Can we allow ourselves our own self-forgiveness whenever we make a mistake or learn a lesson? Do we have limits to how many times we can forgive? Again, it helps to remember that forgiveness has a lot to do with letting go, not holding on to those mistakes, learning the lesson, letting go so you can move on. It's a spiritual ability.

Grounding and neutrality can assist with validating your own unique ability to forgive, so that you're not carrying the weight of all the many mistakes or learning experiences you've created. And forgiveness doesn't mean denying your body's emotions or experience; it's simply about releasing and letting go, allowing things to fall away, so that you can begin anew, in the present.

Who are you having a hard time forgiving? What is it that you're holding on to? How heavy is that burden. Wouldn't it feel great to let it fall away, to finally end the conflict? As you release what no longer works for you, you can get in touch with your own truth, and as you do that, you can create what works for you now.

You are free to partake of the field of infinite possibility.

When you add forgiveness to your prayer or meditation, you create a space for newness to appear. You allow yourself to release what you're holding on to against a situation or person, even if it is yourself. You release the hold and allow the energy to flow. You open yourself up to experiencing the universal forgiveness, which is always available.

If you hold on, it's difficult to allow your own forgiveness or to see that the Universe has already forgiven you. And if you find it difficult to forgive someone else, then it's like the story of the two monks. Essentially you will continue to carry the burden with you, perhaps even longer than the person you're upset with. As you allow forgiveness, you lighten your load. You can allow others to simply be where they are at. You may not agree with their choices, but forgiveness allows you to accept, release and let go, and continue on your own way.

CHAPTER 16

Communication

Communication is something that I have affinity with. This is not news to the people who know me. I have been known to hold a conversation not only with others, but also with myself, at length, out loud, at my desk or in front of the computer. Talking makes my body happy, and as spirit, I enjoy it because it is one way that I can communicate either with another person or with myself.

When I sat down to write this, however, I found I was at a loss for words. The topic of communication was so vast. There are so many avenues, each with its own twists and turns and particular aspects. Even in the limited avenue of words, there are many different languages and associations within those languages, not to mention the different ways we can color what we say by inflection or a look.

We are so creative as spirit, and I believe that one of our greatest drives as spirit beings is to communicate. We do this all the time, consciously and unconsciously. We communicate by what we say, by what we wear, by our actions and our thoughts. We communicate by what we create and how we interact with our creations. As spirit, we communicate with our energy. By simply being, we are communicating about ourselves as spirit.

By using the spiritual ability of clairvoyance (clear-seeing), a psychic reader can see the vibrations we are emanating as spirit and can communicate to us about aspects of ourselves of which we are not consciously aware or at which we are afraid to look. This information can be an incredible healing, because it validates us and what we are saying to the world. Whatever vibration we sing to the Universe, it will respond in kind. Validation can give us the light by which we can see ourselves and actively decide how and what we want to communicate. We bring our experience into the arena of choice, by which we take back our power.

Now this is a planet of dichotomies, and so I am going to deal with another aspect of communication. I've spoken about the communication that we give outwardly, but there is also the communication that we can receive. I was talking to a really enjoyable woman the other day. She said that she believed in God, but she felt she couldn't reach this essence. Her answers were there for her somewhere, she said, but she just couldn't hear them. One of the things that I realized during the conversation was that as spirit, she had much of her attention outside of herself in all her various projects and creations.

It reminded me of myself. And I know that when all my attention is focused outside myself, I find it very difficult to find the answers to my questions. I could see that the reason she couldn't hear her answers from God was that she wasn't there to hear the communication. Her attention as spirit was not within. It would be like calling someone from a pay phone and never coming to your own home (the body) to receive the return calls.

I communicated this to her, and she immediately began to change her energy, bringing more of her focus to herself. It was a great healing for both of us.

I believe that it is from within ourselves that we can communicate with the Infinite Spirit, whether we call that essence—Goddess, God, Tao, Universal Mind, Great Spirit, Allah (the list continues on and on). I believe that we are a part of all that is, and that our temple, the body, is one sacred place that we can experience this communication. And that it is the place that we also experience our internal communion with self, which is in my opinion another aspect of the All.

There are many ways to find this internal divinity. One such way is through meditation, whether that be a formalized type or simply the focusing of attention with the intention of listening to the silence.

By finding that quiet place within, we can hear the answers that we are asking for. The Universal Spirit is always there if we but take the time to see and to listen. Many years ago I was sitting by a river in Washington State. I started looking around, and all I saw was communication from the All.

I saw my questions about striving answered as I watched leaves floating down the river, carried by the current, reminding me not to fight my own flow of learning. I felt the light of the sun that didn't judge me, or want to know how much I'd accomplished.

The Great Spirit is always there, communicating to us all the time spiritually and through our physical surroundings. But it must be we who stop the chatter, perhaps the chatter of words, long enough to listen and receive, so that we can fully participate in the spiritual conversation that is always in process.

CHAPTER 17

Commitment

Commitment can be a very charged topic, but I feel that it's an important magical and spiritual tool, so I'd like to share some of my thoughts and ideas about it. I invite you to read through what I have to say here, try out some of the energy work at the end of the chapter and sit with it for a while. I hope you will find something of value in this work, as I have. Perhaps it will make it easier to use the energy of this concept for yourself and reclaim it for your own, without a lot of past ideas or other people's embellishments tied to it.

This topic came to the forefront of my mind partially as a result of an experience I had a few years ago. I found myself frustrated with a discussion of commitment that came up in one of the groups I attend. The context of the discussion was relationships. Many believed that commitment was overrated and not at all desirable, that you should only be in a relationship as long as it served your needs and bail out as soon as it did not.

I tried to take this idea in context, knowing that the individual speaking recently had some bad relationship experiences, which may have colored the discussion. The conversation did, however, get me thinking.

Life's lessons arrange themselves as they will, some being much less fun than others, no matter how useful they end up being ultimately. This holds true for relationships as well as anything else in life. Personally, I believe we are in relationships for a variety of reasons, and what looks like a good reason to one person will not be for another. I, however, am a proponent for commitment in general and find it a valuable tool.

After the discussion, I found myself unsettled. I found myself asking questions about commitment, and about how we respond to the concept and the word.

How committed are we? Do we give our word and keep it? Do we understand the power in a vow? Do we speak the truth to ourselves and to others? What does commitment mean to us?

People tend to run from the word commitment as they would from ravening wolves. I have found myself, at times, sprinting right along with the crowd. So I asked myself, "How is commitment defined in the dictionary?"

Webster's Online (www.m-w.com) gave me these definitions:

> **1 a:** an act of committing to a charge or trust: as (1): a consignment to a penal or mental institution (2): an act of referring a matter to a legislative committee **b :** mittimus
>
> **2 a:** an agreement or pledge to do something in the future; especially: an engagement to assume a financial obligation at a future date **b:** something pledged **c:** the state or an instance of being obligated or emotionally impelled (a commitment to a cause)

I also looked up synonyms. They were obligation, charge, committal, duty, must, need, ought and right. Yikes! I tried the *American Heritage Dictionary* and got more of the same. The parts about pledging and agreement sound okay to me, but there is so much heaviness about the word, and the whole thing about being committed to a mental institution doesn't paint a particularly rosy picture.

Why do I feel so strongly about the subject? Why would I want to write about it in the face of those odds? Is it just that I like to stir up trouble? Well, yes, sometimes! Is it that my moon is in Capricorn? Well, yes, that is also true.

First off, relationships are really important to me. If I look at life, all I see are varying interactions between people and things and energy. Life is all some kind of "relationship." That is one reason. And commitment figures very largely in relationships.

I also think that we are at a time when, for some of us, the pendulum has swung to the other end of the dichotomy, away from commitment. This swing is in response to a very intense set of obligations in the not-too-distant past. We may be in the position of "throwing the baby out with the bathwater" when we try to free ourselves entirely from those constraints.

But there is something more, too. I think that commitment is a powerful energy and one that we would do well to own and reclaim for ourselves as a magical tool. I also believe that there is a very real spiritual component to commitment, something about how the world works, and faith and magic and manifestation.

If you intend something, that is one thing. But if you intend and also commit to that thing, I think that it is exponentially more likely to come about—that the Universe, in some way, will support it. This doesn't mean it will always happen in the way you intend or look exactly like you think it should. (I think we would all be bored out of our minds if things were that predictable.) But when you put your focus and energy into something and then add solid commitment to it, it is like a bridge or a doorway that opens ways unknown to you. It's like telling God, Goddess and the Universe that you really are serious about it.

I feel that the Universe helps create or gives form to our creations based, to a great extent, on our level of commitment to them. I think that one of the qualities of the Universal Force is ultimate commitment.

I look at the heavens, the planets and how they move, how precise and cyclical they are, to the point that you can predict with reasonable accuracy where everything will be at any specific time. You can pretty much count on the fact that the moon is going to be full and then start to wane. My experience of God (or whatever word you choose) is very much of something that shines through creation as a manifestation of commitment to that creation. I think that to tap into that energy is one way to manifest our desire and intention.

Commitment is akin to faith in some way. The faith allows the commitment, or the commitment allows the faith. That I commit to something means that I have the faith that I can carry it out and be supported by the Universe in that intention, or that some other way will be made clear to me. My faith is supported and strengthened by my commitment, and then the commitment inspires action.

When I make a vow or a promise or some other act that requires commitment, such as making magical vows or committing to take a body in this lifetime and learn and teach the lessons I agreed I would, it sets up a particular energy. I think commitment, like anything else, is an energy—a specific vibration of energy, one that exists in the present moment, and one that opens a way for things to come into being. It is like a gateway. It is the power of choice—not a dead obligation, but an active, vibrant affirmation.

When we don't allow this energy, or run from it, then we are only partially present in any action or decision. Some part of us is held back and is then not available to bring to our actions. The faith is lacking somehow; the "what ifs" are shaking us; we can lose our power to doubt and fear.

The question might be asked, How can you say that you will or won't do something? How can you commit to anything? Good question. I personally think there are lots of ways to do so. Commitment isn't (in my mind) the same as an obligation. It also isn't about being perfect and always choosing "right," or never changing your mind. It is more about being in line with what you truly intend and gather yourself together to do. If you commit, the Universe has the space to act to bring your intention into being. The heaviness of obligation, I think, often comes from the feeling of having to do something you are not actually committed to, and so you experience an internal conflict and general uckiness (the technical term).

One way I think we can get to that energy of being able to commit to what we are doing is through conscious contact with our inner self/Divinity—some kind of alignment by magic, meditation or simply being that gets us in touch with what we want to do, our pure heart's desire, right action or whatever you want to call it. I see that as God(dess) speaking its will to us, moment by moment, in this lifetime, our own will at a higher octave.

From that deep inner knowing of the rightness of something (that for me is the presence of the Goddess or God, whatever the name), from that deep certainly, can come the ability to choose and to commit to the choice easily. It can feel sometimes that that act of choosing is the commitment and that this very action is the one that will bring things into manifestation. It is magic.

My experience shows me that we create and receive based on our beliefs, and that by our commitment we place our beliefs in motion. I also think that the Universe will create itself around us based on where our attention is. It has been said that "whatever you put your attention on increases," and that somehow we attract to ourselves whatever it is that supports our current level of consciousness and beliefs. It follows then that if we are in line with our choices internally, and bring our commitment to them, that we will find ourselves more and more being supported by the commitment of the Universe to us.

This is why I have such strong feelings about the power of commitment. If we do magic, if we pray, if we want to bring something into being, whatever it is, that is going to require some action or input from us in some way.

On the mundane level, if you want to build a house you will have to put the work into building it and the commitment to follow it through, and if at some point you bail on that you won't actually bring into being that particular house. It may mean that you spend either time or energy or money to fund your project when you would rather spend that on something else. When the commitment is there, though, it can allow you to remember why you are doing all this work to begin with, and complete your creation.

In a relationship, it may mean that you find a way to open up to the other person, work through a rough spot or allow vulnerability because you have a commitment to intimacy, or that you show up when you say you will because you have made a commitment to some group.

On the more magical level, I think that there is level of discipline that comes out of committing to your work, your vows or your intention. You may want to create a magical working. I think that intention, attention and commitment are very closely linked to your ability to make that result happen. Your commitment creates the space from which you open up the time to focus your attention and direct your intention. It may manifest as the time you use to do the work, or the time you spend honing your skills at developing and managing your energy. I think there is some aspect of integrity that comes into play as well.

> Integrity: noun [from Middle English integrite, from Old French, from Latin integritâs, soundness, from integer, whole, complete]
>
> "The quality or condition of being whole or undivided; completeness."

Soundness, whole, complete, honesty, these are things that I personally find closely linked with being able to commit to ourselves. While integrity and commitment aren't the same things, to me they are closely linked. When one can make the commitment to self, the inner spiritual self, then one's actions will play that out, and there is an integrity that comes from all the pieces within oneself melding into a whole. I think that there is great power in this ability to come from that wholeness and bring commitment to it. That is a place from which powerful magic springs.

If we choose commitment, we are left perhaps with wanting to be able to commit to the actions at hand, to bring more of ourselves to our choices. But we still feel haunted by the fear of obligation or of outside influences that we connect to the idea of commitment. This is where the act of reclaiming this energy becomes important. What I mean by reclaiming, in this instance, is to take back the word and the vibration and clean off some of the heavy energy associated with it so that we are not controlled by it. If we see commitment only as something that brings unwanted pain, obligation and mental institutions into our lives, then we will not be able to use it effectively. If it feels like it only creates a prison, we will not be able to see the freedom it can offer. There are many ways to achieve this freedom; I am going to offer one.

The following meditation will help you to "de-energize" the word commitment so that you can begin to get a clearer sense of what the concept means to you in present time, allowing you to reclaim the power of this idea for yourself. This process, by the way, can work with any concept that you would like to release unwanted energy from. Feel free to play with this on your own and see what options you open up for yourself. Enjoy!

Technique

- Begin by grounding and centering. Get comfortable and begin to own the safe, neutral place in the center of your head, where you can be in your body and retain your spiritual perspective. Feel yourself connected to the deep earth and let the warm gold energy of the sun wash over you. Breathe and release.

- Now take a moment and be aware of the idea of commitment. Notice how your body responds as you do so. Do you notice tension or discomfort? Release it down your grounding; use your breathing to assist that process.

- Continue to focus on your concept of commitment. Where did you learn about it; who taught you about it? Use your grounding, and begin to release anything that doesn't belong to you. Release it down your grounding. Release anything that is no longer serving you in the here and now. Breathe as you do this; notice how your body responds.

- Check your grounding, and settle yourself into that comfortable neutral place in the center of your head. With your eyes still closed, create a mental image of the word commitment out in front of your forehead about 6 to 8 inches. Now destroy that image by letting it explode like bright fireworks, or burst like a bubble (or any other way that works for you). Create the word again in a mental image out in front of you. See it. Commitment. Then destroy it once again.

- Keep doing this over and over again, while continuing to breathe deeply and release energy down your grounding. Notice how your body responds, how you feel emotionally. You may find yourself feeling lighter. Continue the meditation until you feel a change, and get to a place where you feel complete for now. Check your grounding. Breathe. Own and reclaim commitment for yourself as spirit in this present moment.

- When you are done, open your eyes, bend forward and touch your hands to the floor, as you relax your neck and release any built-up energy around the head and shoulders into the earth. Slowly sit back up. If you journal, this would be a great time to record your experience.

Section Three
Further Energy Work

Clarity

The glass is pink, it shatters in the moonlight.
You can see it as it falls glistening and soft like snow,
but sharp with its edges thin and fine from the breaking.

It is so light
that the separate pieces are caught by the currents in the air,
warmth holding them aloft,
a flurry of pink stars glittering in changing constellations,
or a flock of tiny angular birds with the sunset on their wings,
gliding with singular purpose
cool air calling them to the earth.

So much beauty from this explosion in the night,
and you wonder at the strength that held this glass together
at the power released from its breaking
and at the color which through the moonlight is shown,
even now, reflecting off the glass.

Another change, you think
as you watch what's left of the lenses drift away
like wisps of rose-colored smoke.

The frames fall silently to the earth
empty and clear with the whole world passing through them.
And part of you wonders how things will look
in the true color of day
and part of you has always known.

—Erika Ginnis 1989

CHAPTER 18

Dreams

In this chapter, I am going to talk a little about dreams and dream work. I first want to mention that there is a great deal of very good and more detailed information out there than I am going to touch on here. As is usually the case, my intention is to provide you with some (I hope) useful information and a couple of practical techniques that you can begin to use right away if you wish.

I do want to state up front that this is a trickier area of work than some others, and I am not going to go into a huge amount of detail. I have found too often that people would rather learn about dreams or astral work than to address very real waking issues in their lives.

In my opinion, it is more important to become conscious of how you are working with energy in this plane, and to learn to express through your physical body to some extent, before you begin to work heavily in dreams. In reality, I think the two things go hand in hand; however, it is too easy to work on having dreams of being happy, or winning the lottery, or having that perfect relationship, without ever bringing them back into the physical realm.

Having said that, let's not underplay the power of the astral plane or dreams in general. They are very real states of existence; learning about them is an integral part of spiritual work. My opinion (and again this is my personal opinion, and there are many, I am sure, who have differing—but equally valid—opinions) is that it is too easy to get caught up in them if you are not firmly grounded in this dimension.

Ignoring the dream state or undervaluing it is equally nonproductive. So again, the idea of balance comes up. We work on dichotomies in this reality, and here is yet another one. We work with balancing spirit and body, light and dark, dreams and waking.

Dream work is energy work like anything else; the dream state is, however, a slightly different environment than the one we may be used to dealing with. I am going to break down the dream state into three basic areas:

- ✧ Dreams that are part of our bodies' natural need to process information not cleared during the day.
- ✧ Symbolic internal work.
- ✧ The astral plane.

Ever had the experience of doing some repetitious task during the day and then dreaming about it all night? I can remember when I was a child I went berry picking one summer. I picked strawberries all day. When I closed my eyes on the bus on the way home, all I saw was strawberries! When I went to sleep that night, I spent the entire night continuing to pick strawberries in my dreams. I woke up feeling tired the next day and very sick of strawberries.

This experience is an example of one aspect of the first kind of dreaming that I want to cover. It is the kind where our bodies are trying to process things that we did during the day.

We take in information through our senses while we are awake. Usually, we process this information somehow before we go to bed. When we do not have the time or take the time to process what we need to from our daily lives, then we will often times carry that into our dreaming state.

You can think of parts of your mind as being similar to a computer. Sometimes, our dreams are nothing more than that part of the mind dumping large amounts of extraneous data. While this is important for our minds to do, I have found this to be a particularly tedious aspect of dreaming. Another example of having your mental "buffer" full is when you lie in bed for hours trying to sleep but can't because you are going over some past or future stressful situation. Then if you do fall asleep, you find yourself continuing that same train of thought, endlessly going over something that in reality you would really rather put to rest (so to speak).

The answer to keeping this kind of dreaming to a minimum is to find some way to clear your mind before you go to bed. Meditation (are you surprised I mention this? ... I thought not) is a great way to do this. Meditating a little while before bed can clear that mental data so you can go on to do other things in your dream time. You can also accomplish this by taking a little time to relax before bed, perhaps letting your mind wander a bit, staring at the wall, letting your thoughts settle.

I have found that if I can't sleep, or if I keep replaying some unwanted event in my mind, that I can let it go if I get back up out of bed and give my mind time to process whatever it is. I do this by meditating, but as I said there are other ways to do it as well.

Not all the processing that happens during dream-time is tedious by any means. Dreams are a way that we process things and come up with ideas and answers that draw from the rich depths of our wisdom not always available to our conscious mind. This is very valuable indeed. The kind of processing that I think we are better off without is the kind of "mental noise" that happens when we rush into sleep at the same pace we may have rushed through our day.

The next aspect of dreaming that I want to mention is what I think of as "symbolic internal work." This is the kind of dream that is filled with a lot of symbology. There is of course cross-over in all these aspects of dreaming, but in this kind of dream state, you are working as spirit in a symbolic form. As spirit, we actually work a great deal in symbols, since they carry a lot more information than spoken language.

These are the kinds of dreams that you can get a great deal of information from interpreting. We can tell ourselves things that we won't deal with in waking life; we give ourselves clues to the puzzles that sometimes confound us. An aspect of these kinds of dreams is to not take them too literally. See what the symbols mean to you; meditate on them. Writing these kinds of dreams down can really help make sense out of them. I know for myself that there are times I don't understand what I am being told in a dream until I put it on paper. Somehow the act of getting it out of my head and onto the paper makes things really obvious.

Many times, the fruition of a ritual will come to me in the form of a symbolic dream. One of the differences between this dream form and others is that, while sometimes there is specific astral working involved, usually it is a more internal process. It is deep internal spirit work. This does not make these dreams any less important than what we may think of as "astral" adventures, especially if you take into account that there are those that say that the entire universe is contained within. However, it is good to be able to have a sense of the difference, if for no other reason than to be able to differentiate when that dream with cousin Mabel is really cousin Mabel communicating with you, or whether you are using cousin Mabel as a symbol of something else. This can prevent the odd dynamic that can come from confronting someone because you had an unpleasant dream with that person in it, when in reality he or she didn't have anything to do with it at all. You may laugh at this, but I have seen it happen.

This brings us to the last aspect of dreaming that I want to mention. It is the one that I hear mentioned the most when we talk about dreams. This is called the astral plane. Now there is so much information about this single subject (much of it conflicting) that I hesitate to say much about it at all. But since I do have this propensity to chat, I will of course go on. The astral plane is a dimension of reality that is just one level up from where we spend our time when we are awake. It is slightly less dense vibrationally than this physical world but not greatly so.

It is a plane of existence associated with the Earth. It is one of the places that we go when we dream, when people speak of lucid dreaming, this is usually the plane of which they are becoming aware. It is a very handy place to work as spirit. On the astral plane, there isn't the same kind of responsibility for your actions as there is here on the physical.

That isn't to say that there isn't any responsibility, just that it is different. When you go shoot someone in a dream on the astral plane, you haven't actually done the same action as if you brought that action back into the "real" world. In some ways, it is a lot more like animation; it's a bit like that Coyote in the Road Runner cartoons, who kept falling off cliffs and getting blown to bits and getting anvils dropped on him over and over again. As you may remember (and I realize that I may be dating myself here), he keeps popping right back up as if nothing happened and starting all over again. The astral in some ways is more analogous to the experiences in a good animation cartoon.

(I am in some ways oversimplifying here, since there are instances where an altercation on the astral can affect your energy. I don't want to go into this here, but suffice it to say that if you have a particularly unpleasant interaction on the astral, a bad dream, it is always a good idea to meditate and do a little cleansing healing work on your energy when you wake up. It takes some amount of time for something to translate from the astral to the physical so you can avoid a lot of annoyance by simply taking the time to clear your energy, aura, chakras etc. when you get up in the morning.)

The astral is very handy for us as humans. We are working through time and space here on the earth. The astral plane handles time and space completely differently. Have you ever noticed how you can have something that feels like an entire lifetime happen in a dream that takes no more than the 10 minutes or so that it takes your snooze alarm to reset in the morning? Also, we can work on the past or the potential future on the astral. Many times, people use the astral plane to heal old emotional wounds or try out a potential future and see if it is something that they really want to create in their lives.

This brings up an important point. The futures that you see in the astral are not set yet. You do not have to experience or bring into your life an event simply because you lived it on the astral plane. There is free will. A wise monk once said that *any* unpleasant event that has not yet come to pass, is avoidable. This applies very well here.

The same, however, is also true with things that you experience on the astral that you do want to happen. Just because you win the lottery on the astral does not mean that you will necessarily have that experience in your waking life. This is one reason why many magical traditions tell you to take some physical action after you do a particular working. The purpose is to bring the energy into the physical. Otherwise, you may get what you want, but it will stay on the astral plane, which is all fine and good but doesn't really do much in the way of—say—paying rent.

When you have visited some experience on the astral first, or have met someone on the astral before meeting them in person, you may have the very real sense that you remember the experience from somewhere else. It's as if you had already been there and done that. Well, guess what? You did.

Now you may be wondering how to tell whether something is an astral experience or not. For some people, it is very obvious because they have had what is referred to as an out-of-body experience. This is an experience where the person has a conscious awareness of leaving their physical body. You may have also heard of it as "astral projection", the conscious act of taking the astral body out while the physical body is at rest. Most of us have an awareness of our physical body. What some of us do not know, however, is that we also have what's called an astral body. This is a less dense body that we use when we go out dreaming at night and want to work on the astral plane. We have more than this astral body as well, but I will not be going into it here.

One of the coolest examples of what an astral body looks like, I remember, comes from *Return of the Jedi*. At the end of the movie there was a shot of Yoda, Obi Wan Kenobi and Anakin Skywalker (previously Darth Vader), all watching the festivities. These are all characters that have "died" at some earlier point in the *Star Wars* epic. You see them in their original bodies (this is especially notable with Anakin Skywalker), which are transparent to some extent and have an electric blue glow around them. When I saw this in the movie, I remember noting that someone had done their homework.

The astral body often has a characteristic electric blue glow around it. It normally looks like us, but not always. Sometimes people can appear as other people in dreams, and lots of people alter their astral bodies to look "better," taller/shorter, thinner/heavier, younger/older, etc., than they may appear in "real" life. I mention this just in case you meet the man/woman of your dreams, in your dreams. They may appear slightly more "flawed" when you meet them in person... I of course would never do something like that myself.

Another way the astral can differ from other dream experiences is that very often it feels just like you are awake. Even if there are elements in the dream that are out of the ordinary (that unicorn in the corner, say), you still feel like it is exactly like your waking life. One of the reasons for doing lucid dreaming is to have a way to bring your awareness to the fact you are "dreaming" without coming back to your body.

Flying dreams are very often astral experiences. I can remember vividly a dream where I was flying. I found myself being conscious that I was on the astral (by using a technique I will mention later) and looked down at my body. I was amazed at the vibrancy of the blue that surrounded my astral body; it made quite an impression.

Sometimes, when you come back to your body after an astral experience you can hear a strange "whooshing" sound and almost a "pop" as you come back in. This can happen especially when you come back rather abruptly.

One thing to remember about bringing information back from the astral is that you can't always count on each fact verbatim. There are a couple of different reasons for this. One is that we bring the information back into our bodies through our own personal filters. This will color the information. If we see something on the astral that we have no concept for, we may choose the next best fitting concept to make it make sense to the body. This is a good argument for doing cleansing and clearing work on our energy in general so that we can bring back spiritual information with less baggage attached.

The other thing that can affect what we remember is that sometimes in order for us to bring something back into the body we sort of "alter" it or attach a "lie" to it, so that we can remember it. This may make more sense if you think about how very volatile those insights you sometimes get are. If you don't write them down, they tend to fly right out of your head. There are those that say that this is a planet of many illusions and that spiritual truth has a hard time hanging around. If that is the case, as it may be, then it makes sense that we have to alter things just a bit to bring them into this physical reality. So that dream you had with Cousin Mabel (remember her?) comes back to the body as a dream with a unicorn with Cousin Mabel's voice.

Our job is to decipher what the truth is from the lie (a handy definition of clairvoyance by the way) so that we can have the information that we wanted access to from our astral experience.

So there are a few things to think about when you deal with dreaming. I will close with some ideas about how you can start to get more in touch with your dreams and astral experiences.

As with everything, I suggest that you spend time meditating and grounding daily to get in touch with yourself and your own energy so that you can enjoy what you are creating both here and in the dream time.

Technique

- As with all energy work, I want to emphasize grounding as a way to be safe, be in charge of your energy and become more conscious of what you are doing. Start with grounding before you go to bed. While you are in bed, also ground yourself. Don't let the fact you are lying down throw you, because grounding can be done in any position. Being grounded while you are out of the body is one of the surest ways to feel safe when you are out interacting with the different energies and beings you run into during a given night.

- Make a conscious agreement with yourself that if you run into anything that is not beneficial while you are out traveling that you will immediately return to your body and wake up, even if it is briefly. If for any reason you find yourself dealing with something unpleasant, remember your grounding. Turn and face what it is and ask for whatever gift it has for you, then tell it to go. This may seem simple, but try it sometime and see what happens. You may be surprised.

- As you are grounded and falling asleep, make a conscious decision and agreement with yourself about what you are going to be doing while you are out of your body—something like, "I am going to do healing work on (fill in the blank) tonight while I am out of my body."

- You can work on whatever you want. You can get ideas for new things, solutions for existing problems, heal physical pains. Make an agreement with yourself each night. It may take time, but if you stick with it, things will come to you.

- Having a journal by your bed is a great way to start to get more in touch with your dreams and astral experiences. It is important to write the stuff down when you first wake up though, because the images will fly right out of your head.

- One last thing I want to leave you with is one way that I have used to become more conscious in my astral experiences. I believe it came from a metaphysical book I read years ago. The idea is to start to tell yourself that you will look at your hands in your dream, and when you do you will remember that you are dreaming. This is a very simple thing and very hard as well. It will take time, but keep saying that to yourself and over time it will sink in. At some point you will be in a dream and look at your hands and—voilá—you will become conscious that you are not in your body. What you do from there is up to you.

CHAPTER 19

Divination

I have thought about divination for years, not only because I personally want to know what is around the corner sometimes, but because I have worked with energy and as a clairvoyant since the early 1980s (hmm... I must have started at age 2, otherwise that would make me *how* old?!). One of the things I get asked a lot is whether clairvoyance (the type of reading I use in my practice) is foretelling the future.

I think that the answer depends on who you ask, but for me I define clairvoyance simply with a translation from the French, as "clear seeing." I always tell people when I do readings for them that I will give them information mostly about the energy and circumstances in the present and not predict the future.

I do so because of the way I was trained to read and also because of my belief that we have free will and can alter our paths to a large extent by our choices. "Free will versus fate," simplistically put, can be argued from either side, and I have to say I can see value in both points of view. While I believe we are at choice, I also believe that the greater capital "I" of us may be at a higher level, making choices of which we are not always consciously aware, and the result can look a lot like "fate" or "luck."

I also think we set some ideas up prior to birth, a lesson-plan or playing field. That's where astrology fits into things for me. If I want to see trends far in the future, I look to astrology and the transits that are taking place, or the progressions. I find that astrology is one of the most accurate ways to get that kind of broad view into what is unknown to my conscious mind about the lessons I have chosen.

Other types of divination can put us in touch with aspects of ourselves and the Divine (hence the word) that we may overlook in everyday life. While I don't generally read the energy of someone else's future, I will often use meditation or some form of divination to get a deep sense of where I personally am at a given point in my life.

Wonderful tools exist out there to get in touch with what we are seeking. The caution, in my opinion, is to remain mindful of the source and not become dependent on particular tools to the extent that we forget that each tool is simply a pathway to inner knowledge or the Divine. It can be easy sometimes to lose the essence by focusing on the tool. You can also then miss the wisdom that is around you all the time. The statement "I have to have this particular amulet or I can't know what's right for me" is very limiting.

I have heard it said that you can use anything to gain insight into an issue, opening a book and reading a random paragraph, seeing how the ripples fan out across a mud puddle in the street or watching the changing shape of a flock of birds. Whether you can use such things has a lot to do with your state of mind and how you view things around you. If this reality is all in some way a manifestation of the Divine, then if one is tuned into that source behind and inside all, one can use whatever is at hand. It's like swimming in a sea of information, or like walking through a field of computer terminals all connected to an amazing network, depending on your paradigm.

Even with all the work I have done in this field, I still find myself amazed that this stuff works! As an example, a few years ago I played with a great computer program called "The Oracle of Changes," which throws the Chinese oracle the I Ching. I found myself surprised that the program would be accurate. Then I started thinking along the lines above, and I started to wonder how anything wouldn't work for divination! As if God/Goddess/the Divine would exist everywhere except my computer! So much is about perspective.

When I was meditating a while back on divination and the tools I use, I came across a new perspective I'd like to share. As I mentioned earlier, in my practice I generally use my clairvoyance to do whatever kind of "divination" I do. I normally don't think of my practice as divination at all, because I have thought of divination as the act of foretelling the future, and I don't put much focus on the future. What I do when I read is to look at energy and bring into conscious awareness information not otherwise available to the person I'm reading for. So, in a way, my reading is a type of divination. Also, one might ask, "What constitutes the future?" Is it "more" future if it is 20 years from now or 20 minutes from now? These were the kinds of things I asked in my meditation.

When I read, I adjust my energy so that it is vibrating at a slightly higher level than that of the person I am reading. This adjustment allows me to tune in to information that hasn't quite manifested on the physical plane yet but is just coming into being.

I suppose this practice actually is reading the future, the future just beginning to manifest—creations always start at the spirit level first. Free will comes into play here, since I believe that you can change your future based on your beliefs and the choices that you make in the present.

One thing I was profoundly moved by when I meditated on these things was the question whether there is any "future" at all. I believe that everything is happening all at the same time and that we have this particular "time and space" area of reality set up in which to learn things. When I started really looking at what I do when I read and how I adjust my energy to find what I am looking for, and why that works, I came up with some very interesting insights.

I got that past, present and future, which we normally visualize as on a horizontal time line, might more accurately be seen as on a vertical vibration line or spectrum. The lower/slower vibrations correspond to the "past," and the higher/faster vibrations correspond to the "future." When I raise my vibration slightly to read the energy someone is just beginning to manifest as spirit, I am putting myself in that person's "future" to take a look. It of course looks like my "present."

In my yoga class, my instructor is always saying that we are the past tense of God or Goddess (or whatever word you choose), and that God is who we are in the future. I am actually beginning to get what that is about, and it is the same concept.

What I see we are doing with meditation, magick or prayer is raising the vibration in the body over "time and space" toward some culmination point where time and space cease to exist in this linear form. In fact, the idea of "raising energy," as we do in a ritual, works great with this idea, because raising energy puts the thing that we want to happen into this higher energy level and hence into our "futures," so that we can catch up to it later in our body's reality - in other words, manifest it. As we increase our vibrations, we decrease the time it takes to catch up with our creations.

In my own practice, I talk about present time a lot, as being the point of power. The importance of working from present time also holds true because the present is where our bodies operate, since that is where they exist. When we work in present time, we can do our energetic work and be in alignment with the body, allowing it to evolve through its cycles and staying present with our energy to be able to respond as spirit.

If we fall back into "past time" (with unforgiveness or blame especially), depression can hit, since our energy is falling back into a slower/lower vibration. Also, if we as spirit jump headlong into the "future" (with worrying or being two steps ahead of ourselves) and try to take the body there, the body will stress out and get very fearful, since then it is trying to vibrate at a rate higher than it can at the moment.

The more that we, as the magickal, spiritual energy beings that we are, allow ourselves to harmonize with the body by matching our vibrations in alignment with the body's "present," the more we can draw our bodies and personalities up in vibration over time, and ultimately get to that experience of the unfolding moment.

I see that this gentle drawing up of our vibration into the future (which already in reality exists) is the goal of my kind of divination. I accomplish this drawing up by continuing to clear my own field by meditation, and also by the release I get from reading other people. This process is somehow cumulative; at some "place" in the "future," we are all one thing. So whenever any one of us assists another to draw themselves up, by divination or healing or anything else, then in some way we each get lifted.

I have found this a very valuable idea to meditate on. I knew it to be significant information when it came to me, and then I promptly forgot it! The exercise of writing this chapter brought it back to me so that I could get it down on paper.

I know I have more to do along these lines. I am looking at all that I do in new ways. As I do my own magick, and meditate and teach and generally live my life, greater possibilities present themselves. Or, probably what's really true is that I can see what was already waiting for me, which is just another form of divination.

CHAPTER 20

Kundalini

Kundalini is a very powerful, transformative energy that has been used for centuries for growth, enlightenment, sexual enhancement and healing. Sometimes pictured as a snake rising up the spine (like the medical symbol used in Western medicine), it has been referred to as a divine fire.

You may have heard of it in relation to yogic or sacred sexuality practices. While Kundalini is not the same energy as sexual energy—I will go into detail about this later—it is often used in conjunction with sexual energy and sometimes even confused with it, since Kundalini can easily turn on during orgasm.

Kundalini energy alone can be quite compelling, and it can sometimes be overwhelming if you aren't prepared for it. One of my teachers long ago said she had met people who'd thought they had fallen in love with someone, when it was only their Kundalini turning on while with them! Kundalini is an energy of healing, change and transformation that spiritualizes the body.

It is actually a body energy itself that originates from the first chakra. What I mean by "spiritualizes" is that as you run it, it takes the energy and pictures stored in the body, and over time raises their vibration and frees the energy from that state. I'd like to review the quotation (mentioned in chapter nine) from Indian yogi Paramahansa Yogananda because it relates to this process as well:

"As water by cooling and condensation becomes ice, so thought by condensation assumes physical form. Everything in the universe is thought in material form."

In keeping with that analogy, you might think of Kundalini as one of the ways that energy gets warmed up into a less "material" form. This warming is a process some refer to as enlightenment, which is one of the reasons people meditate. As you raise the vibration of your body, clearing and cleansing it of denser energies, you will be able to bring more of your own energy and awareness as spirit into and through your beautiful physical form.

People have used Kundalini to handle intense energy, such as sexual energy or intense emotions. I was taught that many orders of monks, especially Eastern monks, run Kundalini energy. One of many reasons is because it is very satisfying to the body and helps with celibacy. It is also the energy associated with those stories about yogis being able to withstand the mountain cold or melt snow and ice. The energy itself when run gently can also clear out blocks to its running. It is associated with movement; the body likes to move in some way when running it. My guess is that it also stimulates endorphins, the body chemical that produces the "runner's high," although I have no scientific proof of this.

Raising vibration may not be how you think about Kundalini. When I was growing up, I heard about Kundalini, but it was always shrouded in mystery and sometimes fear. I heard stories of people having injured themselves using it, that it was dangerous to use and that you had to have numerous years in some hidden school to gain access to it. There are reasons for this aura of concern around this energy. It is very powerful, it runs through specific channels, and you can indeed do damage if you don't know what you are doing or try to crank it on all at once. You may not have anything bad happen to you, but it is always best to learn what you are working with before doing the work. Be warned also that you will certainly start profound change by working with Kundalini, and that this change is not trivial.

The good news is that you can learn to use Kundalini energy consciously and gently to great benefit to you and others. It can be a wonderful addition to your personal meditation. When you get it running smoothly and gently, Kundalini feels fabulous! The body loves this energy. It makes it really easy to meditate for extended periods of time, and it can help you handle and process those more difficult vibrations that we are all faced with.

Regardless of whether or not you want to use Kundalini on a daily basis for meditation, I think it is important to know what the energy is and how to work with it to some extent, such as how to turn it off. Knowing how to shut Kundalini down can prove useful if you're running it unconsciously, for example.

This energy often runs in the body all by itself under specific circumstances, but we don't always recognize it. It often turns on when you are ill. It is associated with the fever that helps kill germs in your body. People also often run it at night while sleeping, since it is used to help process information and rejuvenate the body. People who do this get very hot to the touch in bed. If you wake up really hot and sweating, chances are you have been running your Kundalini while dreaming. When you start to work with it during waking hours, you may have to retrain your body so you don't immediately want to go to sleep when you start meditating.

If you ever get insomnia and you are all hot and bothered—not in a good way—that can also be your Kundalini running rampant. A number of other physical problems can be traced to Kundalini running improperly in some way, including headaches and unexplained skin rashes.

Hot flashes are also usually connected to an experience of Kundalini energy. As the female body is shifting its focus biologically from mother to crone, a process that happens whether or not we want to have children, we as spirit in female bodies shift spaces. We move from a physically creative space, preparing each month to create a new body for some lucky spirit, to a more specifically spiritually creative one, moving toward menopause. It's a time of shifting energy, and Kundalini often kicks in to facilitate this process.

Unconscious Kundalini isn't all bad. When you get chills up your spine, it can be Kundalini running. Sometimes, certain music will set it off. Very often, spiritual experiences will pop it open, such as being in circle, in a church or in the presence of great art.

The main problems with Kundalini happen when this energy isn't run through the channels it prefers or when it hits a block in a channel while running too intensely. In either case, Kundalini can flow out into other areas that can't handle that energy directly. One analogy is to think of how useful electricity is when it runs through wires, and how unpleasant the alternative can be.

Although many types of energy can move anywhere through the body and be just fine, Kundalini runs most happily through either the main channel (the spine) or the secondary channels (which run up the legs and down the arms and connect to smaller channels that run on both sides of the spine). You can run Kundalini through the chakras as well, but I won't go into that in this book.

In addition to using the right channels, it is incredibly important to be grounded when you use this energy—think back to electricity again. Grounding helps your body to work safely with higher vibrations of energy. It also helps your body release and process the energy that is stimulated by the healing power of Kundalini. At the end of this chapter, I will give some short guidelines on how to ground, how to clean the channels for Kundalini and how to turn the energy on and off.

When you use Kundalini energy in meditation, letting the body run it for at least 15 minutes at a time is important so there is time for it to get moving. It is helpful to keep your spine straight, so the energy can run easier. Remember to keep breathing; your breath will assist how the energy flows. Drink a lot of water; you will dehydrate faster when running Kundalini. Consider taking a shower or sponging off when you are done if you have been running it really intensely and plan on going out afterward. Kundalini helps to cleanse toxins from the body, and those toxins will come out through your sweat and your skin. Showering can feel fabulous and can also assist to avoid "smelling like a wet dog," as one teacher used to say to her students.

Another thing to bear in mind is that Kundalini starts by clearing out first chakra energies, since it starts running from that chakra and the base of your spine. As I mentioned before, by running Kundalini you begin the process of spiritualizing the body, which starts by clearing the denser energies. Denser energies are the ones that vibrate slower, such as fear, hate, resentment and emotional pain. You know the ones. Don't panic! Don't run and hide! Running Kundalini is worth it. Enhancing your grounding will make everything easier. Plus, you don't have to do everything all at once.

Kundalini is an important component in spiritual evolution. This is true not only for us as individuals, but also for our planet Gaia—our larger body. The Earth itself is going through some big evolutionary shifts, clearing out those same denser vibrations. The energy from the Earth's Kundalini is the energy that runs through the secondary channels in the body. During times of change like these, Kundalini is actually running though the planet and is available to use from that source as well.

Many people are being affected by this changing energy and do not understand it. One thing that happens when you cleanse something is that it gets stimulated first so you can actually clear it. Furthermore, when cleansing we all can forget who we are and identify with the energy we are clearing out. We get drawn into it, into fear and hatred. Remembering who we are and what we are doing spiritually is essential when doing such hard work. Our work is ultimately one of enlightenment and the raising of consciousness. Recall that to help keep from being drawn into denser energies. Let yourself remember the purpose of the work, and consciously prepare your body, then you can comfortably use the Kundalini energy coursing through the very ground beneath you to assist in healing yourself and the planet.

Enough with the fear and hate! I mentioned sexual energy earlier. This energy often is associated with Kundalini, but it isn't the same energy. It feels wonderful, however, to run them at the same time. Sexual energy is a vibration that originates from the second chakra, which often is experienced as a lighter vibration than Kundalini and which can run anywhere in the body just fine. This energy doesn't just have to do with sex; it has also to do also with regeneration, rejuvenation and new life, it's incredibly creative. One way to look younger is to start actively letting your sexual energy run. There is a lot of nature in sexual energy; picture new, light-green leaves and spring shoots coming up through the moist soil. Kundalini can turn on your sexual energy, and sexual energy can turn on your Kundalini; they work well together. You might run each separately and then together to feel the differences. Plus, it just feels good!

On its own, Kundalini when worked with properly can greatly help you get in touch with yourself as spirit. It is a powerful tool that can create dramatic change and transformation. You can learn to use it safely and enjoyably, and it really moves energy. I love it!

Make sure and read through all of the information following before proceeding. That way, you will know how to turn your Kundalini energy off before you turn it on.

Technique

- Find a comfortable chair where you can sit with your back straight and your feet flat on the floor. Then begin by grounding and centering. I strongly recommend getting comfortable with grounding and centering by doing both a number of times before running your Kundalini.

Clearing the Head Channels

- Step one is to clear the head channels. The head channels are connections between eight small chakras located around the head. These small channels can get clogged easily and are one of the most frequent causes of headaches associated with Kundalini. They can be easily cleared by using your index fingers to press on each matched pair of chakras for a few seconds while running your healing energy through them. It feels fantastic!

- Work with the chakra pairs that sit across from each other. The locations of the pairs are as follows: One small chakra lies at each temple. One chakra lies at the small hollow at the back of your head, where it connects to the skull; this chakra matches up with one in the center of your forehead. The last two pairs of chakras are a little harder to find. In the third pair of chakras, one chakra is located on the right between the temple and the middle of the forehead on the brow, a little above the eyebrow; this chakra matches one on the right side of the back occipital lobe, those bones at the lower back of your head. The fourth pair matches the third but is on the left side of the head.

Clearing the Main and Secondary Channels

- Step two is to clear out the main and secondary channels. To do so, as you relax in your chair, grounded and centered, create a mental image of a white rose. This is going to be your "dust mop" rose. Take the rose, and starting from the very tip of the curve of your spine, near the first chakra, clean out the main channel by bringing the rose up through the spine and out the top of your head, allowing it to collect energy and blocks as it goes. Now, using your mind's eye, look at the rose. Has it changed color as it picked up energy? Pop the rose like a bubble to clear the energy. Repeat this process until the rose stays white. Next, do the same process with a gold rose. Remember that it is important to have working channels so the energy runs smoothly.

- After you are done with the rose cleaning, run some of your own healing energy through the channel and allow it to mend any breaks or cracks in the structure. You don't have to know how this happens; you can simply run some neutral, cleansing gold energy through that channel and use your mind's eye to watch the healing take place.

- Repeat the whole process for the secondary channels. These channels run up from the feet, through the legs, connecting on either side of the first chakra with channels that run up along the spine on each side of the main channel and out the top of the head. Where these secondary channels pass up through the neck area, the arm channels begin and run down each arm and out the hands. Draw first a white and then a gold rose through these channels, then run healing energy to mend breaks.

- Once the channels are clear and repaired, recheck your grounding and take some deep breaths. You can now begin to gently awaken the Kundalini.

Kundalini Awakening

- Be aware of your first chakra and the base of your spine, the portion that has that little curve in it at the very tip. Breathe and become aware of that area. Allow the Kundalini energy to very gently begin to awaken. Say hello to it. Take your time.

- Allow it to begin to gradually move up the main channel, your spine. It may move in a slightly spiraling motion. Breathe and ground and allow the energy to gently move.

- With your mind's eye, picture a dial that is marked from 1 to 10. Set this dial at 1, or even at 0.5 if you prefer. This is a great way to direct the rate of flow for this energy. If the flow gets uncomfortable, let it diminish until it feels good again and then keep running the energy gently.

- Let this process continue until the energy flows up and out the top of your head. Breathe and allow it to flow. Notice how it feels. You may find that you are gently swaying a little from side to side. This is normal, as the body likes to move when it runs this energy. Continue to check your grounding and centering and breathing. Allow the energy to run until you are comfortable with its flow.

- Work with the dial at a position of 1 or 2 for a few sessions until you are used to the feeling of the energy.

Whenever you begin to run your Kundalini, make sure that you allow at least 15 minutes for it to flow, or your body may get grumpy with you.

- At some point, you may want to add the secondary channels to carry Kundalini. To activate them, simply become aware of the bottoms of your feet where the channels begin and allow the Kundalini that is flowing in the Earth to gently flow into your body. Allow the energy to gently flow at the same rate as in the main channel, if that is comfortable. Let the secondary channels fill with this energy, and let the energy flow up and out the head, down your arms and out your hands.

- (For those of you who run earth energy and cosmic energy, please note that these channels are similar in placement as those used for running earth and cosmic energy but not the same. You can run earth and cosmic energies and Kundalini separately).

- Allow the Kundalini energy to flow through both the main and secondary channels; let the energy gently clear any things that get in its way. Once it's moving and you're used to it, you can simply let it run and use it as a background energy to your other meditation work.

Turning Off Kundalini

- When you are done and want to complete your session, turn off the energy. To do this, create a ball of ice-blue, cool energy above your head. Allow that ice-blue energy to gently enter the top of your head, flow slowly downward through the channels and begin to cool the Kundalini energy and put it back to sleep. Take your time. Let the Kundalini energy cool, and move it down until it curls back up at the base of your spine/first chakra area, in the case of your main channel, or until it moves out the bottoms of your feet into the earth, in the case of the secondary channels. Breathe and notice the change.

- After you have completed this step, create a large ball of healing gold energy above your head and follow that blue energy with a gold "chaser," down the main channel to cap off the energy at the base of the spine.

- Bring some of the gold down the secondary channels and out the bottoms of your feet. You can also allow some gold energy to run down your arms and out your hands.

- Notice how you feel; release energy down your grounding. Allow your energy to come to a comfortable equilibrium. Make notes in your journal if you have one. Enjoy!

CHAPTER 21

Cleansing, Owning and Blessing a Space

Have you ever walked into a building for the first time and felt right at home? Or walked into an empty room and felt as if someone had been arguing there? Have you been out in nature and gotten a really strong impression or emotion that seems to come from the place or land itself, that seemed to be in the surrounding air?

This feeling or impression, sometimes called vibe or ambiance, has to do with the energy of a place. This energy can affect us, can alter our moods, can lift our spirits or create tension for seemingly unknown reasons. If we are open to the awareness, we may even be able to track how different areas affect us, although to a large extent we may have passed though life reacting to the energy without really knowing why.

A vibe can affect our choices. We may not like the feel of a house, so we move, or we don't go to "that" store because we feel sad for some reason that we can't place.

Everything is energy in some form, and it is all in some kind of interaction. As energy interacts and flows, it can leave a residue or signature. Think of it like the faint smell of a bouquet of flowers, after the arrangement has been taken away. Or the ringing of a chord long after it has been struck. The energy of our life colors all that surrounds us. A thought, a feeling, an experience—all of these things have impact on the world around us. We may or may not be able to personally discern all the nuances that these signatures leave, but they can affect us nonetheless, often unconsciously.

The good news is that we are also able to "color" our surroundings actively and consciously choose to change the vibration of the world around us.

Clearing or Cleansing a Space

Clearing or cleansing is the act of using various energetic and spiritual means to remove and release unwanted or excess energy from a physical place to create an environment that is refreshed, safe and pleasant.

You perform a cleansing because, as I mentioned earlier, energy can be felt. Cleansing and blessing a physical space can bring it into alignment with the intention you have for it. It can make it feel better, be more comfortable, and improve the quality of your life in that space.

On a practical level, cleansing and blessing can be useful if you are buying or selling a home or starting a new project. It is also just nice to clear and bless a space to keep up with the energies that get thrown around in the course of living. In some ways, it is not unlike physical cleaning; it is simply done on a spiritual level.

Bringing conscious awareness to the "feeling" of the physical place you are in is especially important when you are doing magic or meditation or you are working with energy. Your results or your experience will be affected not only by your techniques and your intention but by the "flavor" of the surrounding or residing energy. If in no other way, it will have an impact on your mood and the thoughts that you hold in mind when you are working.

Cleansing is useful not only in preparation for doing spiritual work but also in everyday life. If you move into a new house, you may want to remove the old energy from the previous tenants so that you have a clean slate to work with for your own home. If you are in an argument with someone or have someone actively sending uncomfortable energy at you, it helps to have a way to cleanse that from your reality. Even day to day, we run into situations that are not pleasant, and we would do better to find a way to release them than to carry them with us and influence the rest of our life.

Also, I have found that if you have a particular type of energy around you it can attract other like energy to you either by its presence or by your attention on its presence since what we put our attention on increases. If the energy surrounding us isn't of the type that we want, we can clear this away. By doing this, we are being more consciously in charge of what we are attracting and creating. Clearing and owning a space is the way I normally go about working with setting up the "vibe" or feel in any given place.

Many spiritual traditions use one form or other of cleansing, sometimes called "banishing," before doing sacred work. This can be achieved by different means, such as the use of cleansing water or the mixing of salt and water, or the purifying smoke of incense (such as cinnamon, lavender, or frankincense) or smudging the area (with sage, sweet grass, or cedar), or working with symbols or movements with religious significance or with visual imagery (such as a fire circle of protection) that help move the unwanted energy away. Striking a pure tone of a bell or chime is also a way to set the vibration and clear a physical space.

Once of the benefits with using energy itself to clear a space is that you can do it without having to buy anything or use anything external, which may be preferable in many situations—especially at work, where people may not understand why you want to smudge the office before the big meeting! It also helps if you or someone you are working with is allergic to sage or incense, and it can be done quickly and easily.

You don't have to move the furniture for this type of work. Cleansing and blessing a physical space can be used at any time and with any configuration of possessions. It works with the spiritual or psychic energy of a place.

Like cleaning house, banishing may take more than one pass with the "mop" to get the desired effect. Or to take the metaphor a little further, you might need a stronger cleaning solution depending on the kind of dirt and grime that you are clearing away. In reality, the very act of cleaning a room physically can actually clear the energy from it spiritually and can be used as a type of banishing. The broom itself can be used as a symbolic tool to clear away unwanted energy by "sweeping" the energy away.

In my opinion, the single most important aspect is intention. Your intention will fuel and drive whatever you are doing. The clearer your intention, the more effective the cleansing will be.

I am going to include a few techniques for cleaning a physical space with energy. Before doing any of this work, prepare and clear your own personal space (that is, your energy body) by meditating and being aware of your connection with the Divine. (For more about this, see the chapters on grounding, centering and running energy.) If I am in a large building, I always work from the inside out. First, I clear my own personal space and align myself with my own unique energy, then I work on the room I am in, and then I work on the building as a whole.

Technique

Grounding a physical space

- Ground the room you are in, or the area you are in if it's not a room. To do this, visualize a grounding cord that connects from the floor of the room, building or area and flows down to the center of the earth and connects securely there. It is important to remember that this needs to be a separate grounding cord from the one you use for your own body and space. Keeping the two separate will help keep the energy clear in the room or building you are in, and not have it affect your own energy to do so (very handy).

- Allow energy from the room to release down the grounding to the center of the earth. You may feel an immediate change in the room as you do this. It often will make the room feel calmer and more comfortable.

- Always start with grounding the space you are in so there is somewhere for the energy to go once you move on to the next step.

Next I will include three different ways to clear the space with gold energy. I suggest using them all in turn since they seem to catch different aspects of the energy. I will list them here in the order I often use them, but you are free to use any order you wish.

Technique

Clear the room by using gold energy

Using a gold net

- Create a fine-mesh gold net, and allow that net to start at the very top of the room and move through the room from top to bottom. Allow that net to collect anything that doesn't belong in the space, to move out any foreign energy or anything that would interfere or that is not in harmony with the room vibrating at that gold level. Let the net, along with all the energy it collected, drop down the grounding of the room. You can do this more than once if it feels like the room or building needs it.

Cleaning with a gold rose

- Create a big gold cleansing rose (like an energy dust mop that is rose-shaped) and allow that rose to move throughout the room (especially into the corners, because that is an area where energy likes to collect). Let the rose gather all the energy that doesn't belong there, absorbing anything no longer appropriate or beneficial, and allow the energy to come into the present moment. Move the rose throughout the entire room, and then release it down the grounding cord of the room.

Using a waterfall of gold energy

- Allow a wash of brilliant gold energy to start at the very top of the room and move down through the entire space, so that it is like the room is in the middle of a moving golden sunbeam of light flowing from

> infinity all the way to the center of the earth. Allow this energy to clear and cleanse and raise the vibration of the room.

One thing to remember about this way of clearing space is that you can do this when you are physically in the space, of course, but you can also do this before you arrive. That can be especially useful when you are going to work or to an event where you are going to be distracted once you walk in, and you want to have the energy clear before you get there.

Owning a Space

Owning a space is a technique that I would suggest using after you have done a cleansing. When I say "owning," it can bring up lots of images of the more physical aspects of ownership. This is not what I mean by owning a room. This type of owning is a spiritual technique and has nothing to do with who has the deed to the property. You can own a room even if you *don't* own it. The good news is that it isn't mutually exclusive; with this technique, everyone in the room can own it at the same time, and in fact the more people owning it the better. When you "own" something in this way, you are consciously making it yours as spirit, and as spirit there is no time and space and so no competition about who can own something. It is simply a way of creating a safe space to be in, and it can make a room feel really good.

I recommend owning the space if you want to have a meditation space, or if you want to create a space to do some kind of energy work in. This simple technique can help keep the energy where you set it when you did the cleaning in the previous step.

Technique

- To own a room, first ground yourself and get settled into the center of your head. Breathe, relax and create and destroy some roses to clear your own personal space.

- Move your awareness as spirit from the center of your head to the center of the room. With your awareness in the center of the room, send out an energy cord into each of the eight corners of the room and let the cords connect into those corners. You can think of yourself as a star shining in the center of the room, with your rays going out in eight directions.

- Once you have the cords attached to each of the corners, gather the other ends of the cords in the center of the room and then bring those along with your awareness back into the center of your head. You have now owned the room. Notice how it feels. Create and destroy some roses and release energy down your grounding.

- Once you have done this, simply let it be. You don't have to put a lot of attention on it to maintain it, unless something happens in the space to really disrupt the energy. However, it is nice to own a space each time you want to work in that space, or whenever it feels appropriate. I normally do this prior to doing a reading to help set the energy and keep it at a level that will support what I am doing.

Blessing a Space

Once you have cleansed the space and owned it, you can take the next step and bless the space with your conscious intention. Dedicate it to the highest and best of the work that you will be doing in this space, even if that "work" is relaxing with your family. This act of focus is very powerful and is an effective way to support whatever activity you are planning.

As I mentioned earlier, burning sage (also called smudging) helps raise the vibration of the room and will clear out negative or unwanted energy from it. Burning a blessing incense like Nag Champa or a purification incense like cinnamon can also be used to assist in blessing. Ringing a pure tone bell or chime is also a great way to clear space and set the energy. These things can be used in conjunction with any of the other techniques I have listed.

We interact with our surroundings all the time. Taking this interaction to the next level and doing it consciously can greatly increase your enjoyment of the world you live in.

CHAPTER 22

Altars and Shrines

One of my dear friends once said that my decorating style was "Early American Shrine." I was a little taken aback, so I asked him to elaborate. He said, "Given the opportunity, you will make anything into a shrine or altar. Look around at all your stuff, and tell me if that isn't true. You put candles on either side of everything; you add flowers and incense whenever you possibly can. They are all altars. It's cool. I like it. It's just what you do to anything that will sit still long enough."

I took a look around, and I had to admit he was right. It cracked me up. Since that time, I have come to accept with amusement this tendency to create altars wherever I go. I have even used to it to my advantage, being an energy worker, witch and healer and a creator of spaces both private and public where people congregate. I find that there are a lot of definitions for the word shrine and altar.

My working definition for shrine is a holy place of worship and for altar is a place for something revered, an object or place revered for its associations or history. I use shrine and altar interchangeably, even though they may be slightly different things.

I have a working altar and many shrines. In general, for me a shrine is to something or someone specific, and an altar is for doing some kind of focused intentional spiritual/magical work and may have many images on it. However, I sometimes use shrines to do specific meditative work. The definitions are not worth getting caught up in.

What I really hope you get out of this chapter is permission to explore, develop and enjoy what works for you, call it what you will.

Why place shrines and altars? It makes sense to me to recognize the divinity in us and our surroundings. I love arranging things to add that quality of the sacred. I believe it does many things for us. It speaks to a deep part of us that is below the conscious mind, to the deep ocean of the soul. It calms and delights the prehistoric part of us that is, at this moment, still sitting by a fire and telling the mythic stories that run in our blood—the part of us that is in awe and fear of the dark night, the bright moon and the workings of the world, no matter what we do for our living in the modern day to day.

Shrines and altars also speak, at least to me, of beauty. I feel more connected to a sense of grace and loveliness when I am setting things out in a specific way. It puts me in a place of being mindful and honoring, rather than the place of rushing. It helps to remind me that I am spirit. It gives me a place to focus.

My head has sometimes been known to harass me and say; "Hey, what the heck does it matter that you are placing these things thus and so? They are just things, physical objects; how can that affect anything?" In case you also are plagued by this type of inner dialog (or perhaps outer dialog with spouse, partner or roommate), I will say this: I think there are at least two things at work here. (I will warn you that I spend a lot of time seeing things in pairs of dichotomies. I look at a paradox and get really giddy, since I often see both opposites as simultaneously true, and that is where I often find spirit.)

First, when I take the time to pay attention, when I have an intention and dedicate a space (regardless of the size) to something, it changes me internally. The altar exists inside of me somehow. It creates a mental and spiritual and energetic shift inside of me. This is nontrivial. Some would say that all our experience is really our perceptions of our experience and therefore all reality is actually inside of us. Changing something within us, then, can have a tremendous impact. Whether or not you subscribe to this line of thought, it is easy to see how much our inner stance colors our outer experience.

Second, I think that everything is energy and that when you place your intention and direction onto physical objects you do indeed change them on some level. One way of looking at the world says that everything is part of One Thing, and that everything is just arrangements of energy. So the very act of arranging things with sacred intention is by its very nature divine and imbues an even "greater" concentration of sacred energy into the act and by extension the objects acted upon.

There is the added aspect for an altar or shrine of the energy of a particular god or goddess, or perhaps the fey; we may have direct interaction with all of these as real and tangible. When you create an altar or shrine for a particular energy, being or archetype, you are going to be working with yet another layer of interaction and experience, and I should add, opinion. I know from my own personal experience that I created an altar for

Yemayá with all the various things that she would find sacred. The "odd" thing was that I did this prior to even knowing who she was, what her name was and what she would traditionally have on an altar. She was just very clear in telling me what was supposed to be there.

If you know that you want to create a shrine for a specific god or goddess, I think it is always wise and also great fun to do research before you begin. Find some reference books about the deity you are working with, and find out what kind of colors, objects and symbols are sacred to that deity. You may even find pictures of specific shrines and altars that will give you some ideas. Take the time to meditate on the god or goddess. I believe if you allow yourself to get internally still, you can connect with something within that can guide you in your creation. It can be an amazing experience.

One word of caution: If you get really good at this, please remember that you may not want to or be able to provide every single thing the god or goddess might "suggest" on the altar. Some of them might ask for actual living lions or precious gems, or something else that might not be feasible. The phrase "a picture is worth a thousand words" can come in really handy here. Statues, photographs, artwork, all of these things can give the energy you are looking for without breaking your lease or your budget. Work with the energy gently, and allow it to be an inspiration.

Your space does not have to be dedicated to a particular god or goddess. Choose whatever you want your intention to be. It can be a place of prayer, or meditation. It can be a creative expression, or even an altar to creativity. It doesn't always have to be specific. It can be general, such as a shrine containing items that bring a sense of calm or peace. It may be a fountain or a place in your backyard. You may use your altar for magical workings or for contemplation.

Granted, I look at the world through altar-colored glasses. But I believe we create shrines all the time, even if we are not conscious of it. Sometimes they are for things that we would not really choose to honor. That pile of bills we are ignoring in the corner looks a lot like a shrine to a sense of lack. The television that we arrange our living rooms around is certainly a focus of energy. Is there a mantra in our heads that is saying things that don't really serve us? These "accidental" creations are very powerful uses of energy. I am a proponent of doing as much of what we do on purpose as possible. If not that, I propose we become aware at some point of what the heck we are doing, so we can make choices about how we direct our energy. I believe that we are each spirit. We are part of the divine. We have power. We can create. What kinds of altars do you see around you? Are there ones in your life you would change?

For me, the act of making an altar is part of reclaiming my own power to create or identify sacred space. I grew up with a lot of messages that said that someone else had that power, not me. The first altars I made were difficult for me. I had an internal fear that someone was going to smite me down since I wasn't "qualified," that there was this perfect blueprint I had to follow (which I didn't have) in order to do it "right."

Over time, I have found many powerful traditions each with very specific ways to create and bless a shrine or altar. Such ways come from all religions. They are spiritually valuable to people and as such deserve to be honored and respected. I use many of them. The information has been handed down for centuries because it works. However, keep in mind that these traditions are not the only ways to create sacred space.

Get still and go deep inside of you; find the perfect expression of a shrine or altar that is unique just for you. You don't need someone else's permission. It may draw from a particular tradition or from several, or from none. The act of finding this part of you can be incredibly freeing and validating.

Some altars are transitory for a day or a season or a specific ritual (some would argue that all things in form are transitory, but that is a separate conversation!), and some altars are a more permanent fixture.

When you have a personal altar or shrine that is more or less permanent, it will collect and hold energy—not only from you, but also from the energies you work with and people who see it. This can be a great thing and a powerful element to draw from. Stonehenge comes to mind. Alternatively, a personal altar or shrine can be something you might want to clear out now and again. I often suggest people occasionally take their altar or shrine objects down and clean or dust them or rearrange them. Doing this can keep the energy clearer and more current. It can also simply make room for change on a personal level. It can feel really good to redo an altar and bring it up to date with where we are at in our lives.

This rearrangement may happen with or without prior planning. A few months ago, I got two fabulous cats. One of them appears to love feathers to the exclusion of all else in the material world. This love has prompted me to shift some things on my main altar, for reasons that became obvious each time I had to replace various items from the floor when I would return home. Also, my fountain shrines needed to be moved to a higher altitude so they would not become drinking bowl shrines. Thus, I have learned firsthand something I have often told students in my altar outline from one of my classes: "If you have children or pets, it is wise to consider what the best placement of your altar should be."

I am going to conclude this chapter with that very outline. It presents a few things to consider when creating an altar or shrine.

Please use it if you find it valuable. Please do not take it as a set of rules. There are more than enough of those to go around.

I do have suggestions, however. I would suggest approaching this activity from a grounded and centered place so that you will bring more of yourself, and therefore more of the divine, to it. Bring beauty to your creation; let it shine. I would suggest having fun with it. See what you can do when you add a candle or two to the top of a bookcase, or place some flowers in front of a picture. Perhaps we can start a whole new decorating style.

An altar or shrine can be many things:

- ✧ Place of prayer
- ✧ Place of gratitude
- ✧ Focus of meditation or magic
- ✧ Reminder of self
- ✧ Dedicated to a specific deity
- ✧ Place of peace
- ✧ Expression of beauty
- ✧ Creative expression
- ✧ Sacred space
- ✧ Calming sanctuary
- ✧ Reminder of your spiritual nature

How to start if you don't have one:

- ☯ Choose a space.
- ☯ Define the area using cloth, table, rocks, other. It doesn't have to be flat; it can be a wall shrine (this might be good if you have children or pets).
- ☯ Be conscious of your attention and intention.
- ☯ Start to gather and arrange some objects that have meaning for you, that remind you of your highest, best soul-self, that make you feel good or smile. For example:
    - ❖ Pictures and photos
    - ❖ Plants
    - ❖ Shells
    - ❖ Candles
    - ❖ Incense burner and incense
    - ❖ Statues
    - ❖ Rocks
    - ❖ Crystals
    - ❖ Feathers
    - ❖ Water

If you already have one, here are some ideas on how to work with it:

- ☯ Clean it, or move your items on it, change something about it.
- ☯ Add to it.
- ☯ Use it to commemorate some new phase in your life.
- ☯ Keep your journal there.
- ☯ Make new room for changes in your self.
- ☯ Recommit to creativity or to the deity.
- ☯ Make a new shrine somewhere else. Enjoy!

CHAPTER 23

Clearing Perfect Pictures

Perfect pictures can rob you of many otherwise wonderful experiences. They can keep you from seeing the good that is right in front of you, keep you stuck in the past and get in the way of your being in the present moment. They can seem like ideals that you are trying to live up to, but like the carrot at the end of the stick, they are not something that you will ever reach. This is because perfect pictures (otherwise known as unrealistic ideals) do not exist in this reality. They are constructs built out of our pain.

Perfect pictures are created from painful experiences. They are an attempt at ensuring that these painful experiences will not recur. It's not that these pictures are bad; they just bind up our creative spiritual energy, and keep us from accessing our power in the present moment. They don't work especially well for what we are using them for and tend to create more pain and unhappiness in the process.

To talk about perfect pictures I have to touch on another kind of stored energy, called a pain picture.

When the body and ego perceive a painful experience as life-threatening, information about that experience is stored as survival information within our energy system. This stored information is called a pain picture. The situation where a pain picture is created can be physical or emotional. It may be stimulated by an actual threat or by something that was stored as a threat simply because of our age and the situation.

For example, loneliness can be stored as survival-level information in the body because as babies we actually did need some type of physical contact and attention to survive. Survival is a very serious thing to the body. We may also have past life and race memory information that tells us that we must have approval in order to survive because at one time that was actually true. Somewhere in our cells is the memory that if we are ostracized from our tribe and shunned that we will die out in the cold. This result may not be inevitable today, but there are still energies at play within us that equate social approval with survival. Therefore, if we have been shunned or criticized as a child or young adult that pain may have been given a survival-level priority. This is one example of a pain picture.

Whenever you find a pain picture in someone's energy system, you will also find perfect pictures on top of it that were created as a direct result. They are like Band-aids put on a scrape to protect it from the world.

Perfect pictures are energy. We put them into a form that usually has to do with how something should be, or how we should be—a mental picture of how the perfect situation will look. We add some emotional pain, usually from the past, and voilá, you have a perfect picture. You do not generally create perfect pictures consciously; they are internal and often below conscious awareness. You will often have many perfect pictures for every intense pain picture that you have stored.

The process that creates them goes like this: You have a painful experience, emotional or physical. It is very intense, and you want to make sure that never happens again. So you create a bazillion perfect pictures to make sure that it won't (or so you think). The perfect pictures allow you to feel like you have some level of control in a very out-of-control experience. But what they also do is bind up your energy and keep you from having new experiences and learning new ways to do things.

A classic example of a pain picture: You are riding your bike, and you fall down and hurt your knee. There is an ice-cream truck driving by, and you hear the song being played. Unconsciously, the pain gets stored in your knee and anchored by the song. Years later, you don't know why your knee hurts when you hear a certain song or eat ice cream. Perfect pictures would be all the ideas and beliefs that you put in place surrounding the fall.

An example of a perfect picture that might have been created in conjunction with the fall from your bicycle might be that you have to already know how to do something before doing it in front of anyone, to avoid disapproval and the pain of looking dumb. This perfect picture keeps you from trying new things, or if you do, it creates within you such a level of stress that learning is in itself painful. Other examples might be unexplained anger or fear when you see an ice-cream truck or get involved in some type of physical activity that triggers your body-memory of that bike ride.

Another example of creating perfect pictures that many people can relate to is being raised by parents who didn't get along, and perhaps divorced in a way that created emotional pain and insecurity in you, thus creating a series of pain pictures connected to intimacy and marriage. Your reaction to these pain pictures in turn could create perfect pictures about what marriage "should" be. For example:

- ✧ You create a really big perfect picture of your ideal mate. (This picture is to ensure that you won't ever go through that painful divorce experience again.) This ideal mate picture may keep you from ever finding someone to bond with, or you may be so intimidated by your own internalized concept that you chose partners randomly out of despair.

- ✧ You may create a perfect picture about marriage either as a very good thing that you must do or die, or as a very bad thing that you must avoid at all costs. Remember perfect pictures tend to be extreme.

Perfect pictures also make things complex, which in turn can make it hard to do anything at all. In some cases, an individual can feel frozen and unable to move forward at all, based on the level of perfect pictures that are in operation. This freezing effect especially happens if the pictures contradict each other, since they do not have to make sense to be in place. The more pain we have experienced in our lives, the more opportunities we will have to clear perfect pictures.

Here are some things that will light up your perfect pictures and put them to the test:

- ✧ Children or parents—you may have a lot of very clear ideas about who they are and how they will show up, and chances are they won't conform to them.

- ✧ Pets—see above.

- ✧ Work—your career gives you a great opportunity to create a plethora of perfect pictures about success, achievement, responsibility and self-worth, and also how other people should show up and be.

- ✧ Relationships—you may have your own perfect pictures about the perfect mate and what he or she will look like and or be like, and what he or she should or should not ever say or do. Plus, you can trade perfect pictures—much like baseball cards—with your significant other.

- ✧ Spiritual growth—fabulous for perfect pictures. There is always one true way, and there is a right way to do it! Or, my personal favorite, there is an idea of how far you should be along your own chosen spiritual path. It occurred to me a few years ago that following my path wasn't a race. That one simple idea released untold stress from my life.

- ✧ Writing a book—need I say more?

One of the reasons we can get caught on this whole idea of what "should" be relates to the differences in experience between the spiritual and physical planes of existence. You may have a Platonic ideal as spirit, but when it shows up in this physical reality the ideal can look very different. By the very nature of the physical plane, it is going to be transformed. This reality is finite and transitory and therefore may not to our eyes look "perfect" in the same way spirit does.

However, if we see with different eyes, we can view this reality as absolutely perfect. It is exactly what it is, perfectly. It is not always as we would have it be, but it is perfect in that it exists. Looking at this reality this way, we can see what is so and work with that, as opposed to what we think "should" be so.

When we see what is so, we can make changes. If we are stuck in that perfect picture of "it should already be different," that gives us no room to move and less ability to work from our spiritual power.

Perfect pictures should not be confused with goals and desires or plans. You can have a plan for the future or you can have perfect pictures about the future, and they will operate very differently in your life.

When you have a goal or intention, you put it out there and let it unfold. You can look forward to it with calm certainty knowing that this or something better is coming into being. You may even be surprised when your goal is realized because you may have forgotten it for a while. There is no effort involved. You may even find that the intention shows up but in an entirely different and often better way than you dreamed.

When you have created a perfect picture of a goal or ideal, you will have a tremendous weight attached to it and how it proceeds. It will need to show up a certain way. You may put a lot of attention or obsession on every step along the way and have the need to control every aspect of its progress. You may be impatient and stressed and use a lot of mental effort to make it happen, using your "force of will" for a desired outcome. You may get what you said you wanted, but it may not actually make you happy. It may feel pale somehow and propel you into chasing another version of this same concept. Or perhaps you claim your prize and then spend time fretting about losing it, and create even more perfect pictures about how you should be, how the thing should be or everyone else should be in order to keep all of this energy in place. It can be very tiring.

The concept of expectations also comes up in relation to perfect pictures. One school of thought says that expectations are perfect pictures and that as soon as you create them, you are setting yourself up for disappointment. Another school of thought says that expectations are a way that we create. This way of thinking says that if you have your energy flowing in a way where you expect good, and that is what you look for, good will be drawn to you. If you expect bad things to happen, by the law of attraction you will draw bad things to you. This school says that what we expect and what is normal for us is what we tend to create because that is what we hold in mind. What we hold in mind becomes the shape that reality will take, if we're left to our own devices.

Where I currently stand on expectations is that it depends on how I am using the word. I can use it to mean a belief, or I can use it to mean an unrealistic ideal. For example, I can see what my belief-expectations are, based on what is showing up in my life. If in my life I have a great job but I am extremely overworked, I can look for a belief in me somewhere that says work equals stress. Or, if I see that I have a great partner but there seems to be a consistent level of stress in the relationship, my expectation may be that relationships must be difficult to feel real. Or conversely, I may have an expectation that whatever difficulty that arises will be solved easily or that my needs will be met. If those are internally powerful beliefs, then I will most likely see them occur in my life.

Those are expectations at the level of my beliefs. They may have perfect pictures attached to them, or they may not, depending on the day.

However, if I say that I have to have everything resolved immediately and there *shouldn't* ever be any conflict and if there is then everything is *horrible*, then that may be a perfect picture. When my expectations take form as perfect pictures, they often have something to do with the way things "should" or "ought to" be.

Those of us who are control enthusiasts generally have more than our fair share of perfect pictures. Not that exercising control is bad, but the focus on it to the exclusion of all else creates a very stifling existence. Perfect pictures can bind us up. When we are inundated with them, our lives can start to take on a dull sheen, and we can find ourselves getting depressed, uninspired or overwhelmed. Perfect pictures can create a high level of internal and external criticism because we are looking at everything through our fear and pain. When someone has a lot of perfect pictures stimulated, that person will tend to be easily bothered and frustrated.

When we see others through our perfect pictures, we miss the richness of how they show up in our life. Let's suppose I want to feel loved, and the way I have to feel it is for you to cook dinner for me. Because of a painful experience of not getting nurtured with food the way I felt I needed in early life, I created a perfect picture of "I will never go through this again; I will make sure that I always have this need met in this way." But suppose you don't know how to cook and have no desire to cook for me. I may end up feeling unloved and may even leave you without quite knowing why. I may be missing out on all the other ways I can feel loved that you have to offer, simply because I am looking through the reality I have created based on my own concepts of "perfection." These concepts are very limiting.

This brings me to one very important bit of information about perfect pictures that it took me years to learn and have proven in my own life: They are actually *limitations*, strange as that may sound. They are created out of my previous experiences and so can only be as large as what I have experienced thus far in my life. The Universal force has quite a bit larger idea of good than I do, so if I am able to allow myself to let down my guard and release some of my iron-gripped control of the way things flow, all of a sudden I am experiencing things that I never even knew existed. Life goes way past my own perfect picture of the situation.

We create our perfect pictures out of our own pain and the desire to not re-experience it. They are not grounded in the field of creativity but rather in our desire to control in order to keep our ego from further harm. This control keeps us in our smallness and can box us in. In essence, we box in God. Because we create largely from our own beliefs, once we set those in stone it makes it very hard to experience anything new. Once we start to recognize and gently release these misused Band-aids called perfect pictures, we can open up to greater levels of possibility, experience and life.

It is very easy to get serious when dealing with these configurations of energy, but the trick is *not to be*. To be diligent with a healthy dose of amusement is essential, because when we touch on that light, bright energy of amusement, we are lifted out of our self-imposed restrictions and can see beyond these limitations that we have accepted or created. We remember that we are not any of the pictures we have created and stored. We are spirit, and we do not have to be defined by this energy.

Technique

- To clear (or blow up/dissolve) a perfect picture, begin by grounding and centering, and get your energy flowing.

- Then create and destroy roses, and have the concept that you are clearing whatever limitations and perfect pictures that are currently in your way at this moment.

- You can also take this time to clear perfect pictures about some specific subject.

- Another way to clear perfect pictures is to imagine one in front of you and have it appear like a snapshot or photo.

- Tilt the picture to one side, and take some imaginary scissors and cut off one end.

- Let the energy drain out of the picture, and then let it pop like a bubble. Embrace knowing that any information of value that was bound up in the picture has been cleansed and is now being returned to you as spirit for your use in present time.

More ideas on how to work with perfect pictures:

✧ Try doing something badly—everything worth doing is worth doing badly.

✧ Keep returning to the idea called "Shoshin" or "beginner's mind," a Zen concept illustrated in this quote from Shunryo Suzuki-Roshi: "In the beginner's mind there are many possibilities, but in the expert's there are few."

✧ Let your self be consciously imperfect, and dance with the idea that this could be okay.

✧ Notice what happens to your creativity when you loose it from its bondage.

✧ Consider dropping the idea that other people (or maybe everyone else) has a manual on how to live that you somehow missed out on.

- ✧ Realize that you cannot always tell what is going on inside a person by looking at the outside.

- ✧ Give yourself permission to be wrong.

- ✧ Give yourself permission to change your mind about some long-held belief, or at least entertain the possibility that there may be more ways to look at it.

- ✧ Spend just two minutes a day blowing perfect pictures. Do it for one week, or if you are really into it for one month. See how your life changes as a result.

- ✧ Start a gratitude journal. Write five things you are grateful for in it each day, and see how your focus shifts. Gratitude is a vibration that seems to help clear perfect pictures. When we can find some gratitude about things in our lives, it changes the focus. From there, we can see the good that is always there if we put our attention on it.

- ✧ Forgive yourself and others for being human. Do this over and over again.

Remember, you do not need to get rid of all your perfect pictures at once—that in itself, is most definitely a perfect picture. You can let it be a process and let yourself adjust to the changes that will result. Bodies can take letting perfect pictures go quite seriously, and you won't benefit from an all-or-nothing mindset. In fact, it is more effective to work over time, so you aren't tempted to find others to immediately replace what you clear. When you start to gently begin to clear these limitations, you will begin to allow spirit to flow through your life and experience in a way that you may not have felt in a long, long while.

CHAPTER 24

You Are a Healer

You are Spirit, and you are a healer. I have spent many years pursuing "real." It is why I got involved with the type of healing and energy work that I do; it is why I studied the things I studied. I want something that I can feel, that I can bring richly into my experience. It's the part of me that used to do chemistry married to my inner poet. I want results that are reproducible and yet awe-inspiring.

I first was introduced to the kind of healing I do professionally more than 30 years ago. It was 1979. I was in college, and I was having a bad day. I had a friend who ran into me in the school commons and asked me if I needed a healing.

Now before I go on, I must give some background. This was *1979*. No one in this part of the world had ever heard of things like Reiki or the many different kinds of healing that are household words 27 years later. So my first response was not a resounding yes. It was, "Huh? What exactly do you mean by healing?" I wanted to be very clear about this before I agreed. I wanted to make sure "healing" wasn't a euphemism for "date."

He told me he had recently taken a class and learned to do healings and wanted to practice. I said "Oh, well, cool, let's go." We went up to an empty classroom, and he gave me a 15-minute cleansing of my aura and chakras and energy system—these are all words I would learn later. Whatever words he used were not important.

I had been interested in energy and magic and meditation prior to meeting him. I had read books and done visualizations and even had some intense and mind-opening experiences. But one thing happened that changed everything. When I think back on it now, I can see how that experience altered (or set right, depending on how you look at it) my life path. When he gave me a healing, he kept his hands a foot and a half away from my body. He said he was working with my energy field. What was exceptional for me, the thing that changed my experience forever, was very simple. I could *feel what he was doing*, even though he was not touching me at all. It was *real*.

The fact that it was real, could be reproduced and easily learned, was all I needed. I threw myself wholeheartedly into learning everything I could about healing and energy and reading and teaching. I took every class I could and immersed myself in my training. I teach the same techniques today, along with others that I have come across and things I have learned as a result of using these techniques. They are what you find in this book, to a great extent.

In case you haven't thought of this already, I will put it to you directly. You are learning about yourself as Spirit, learning ways to work with the Truth of who you are, your connection to the Divine whole and how to manifest your energy here in this life on planet Earth. This is a healing process. You are therefore a healer. If I am the first person to mention this to you, let me also be the first to congratulate you!

We are all on a healing journey on this planet, in one form or other. It ultimately doesn't matter if you use the techniques I teach or something someone else compiled. It's all good, and it's all about change and growth. Healing as I define it is change. The amusing and lovely thing is, it is really about changing into what you already are, which is Divine, Perfect and Whole.

CHAPTER 25

On Healing and Personal Power

In order to do anything, we need to use energy. We can think of using our energy as accessing our power. Healing energy is one way that this power and energy can manifest. Healing is dynamic, not stagnant; it has movement to it. In order to accomplish that movement, we need to have a working relationship with our own personal power. We do not heal by being weak or passive, and indeed it may take a lot of power to stand strong when we are changing something in our lives that has been in place a long time.

Personal power also plays a role when we run up against other people's ideas about how we should be. If we have been a certain way for many years and we start to heal that, not everyone in our lives will like it. When we change, we automatically create change for the others in our lives. That change can be dramatic or subtle; either way, it takes strength and power to be certain of who we are and to welcome people into the new structure, or to let them move on from us if that is what happens.

I personally believe that healing happens from the inside out; it is all self healing of one kind of another, and usually has more to do with letting go and coming into equilibrium than anything else. I believe that at some deep spirit level we are part of a greater whole that contains the blueprint of ourselves at optimum flow. When we let go and release, we can allow the energy to come into alignment with that blueprint and healing happens.

When we "heal" other people, I think that we do the most good when we assist them and not try to do it for them. This to me looks a lot like shifting energy so that movement and change can take place and then reminding them of what they know at some depth of themselves, giving them permission to continue the process at their own rate of growth.

One the biggest challenges I see healers (including myself) face is to remember to heal themselves first and then continue to do so. It can be easy to fall into being overly responsible for the people you are healing in your life. In reality, we can never fix someone else no matter how hard we try! We can offer and give assistance and help and support and move energy and many other wonderful things but we can not carry another person on their path.

Sometimes it's difficult when we see someone learning their lessons and feel that we could save them so much trouble (since we know so much better from having gone that way ourselves). Our life experience can certainly be useful to people, but only when they are ready for it and not before. Even then our answers aren't necessarily someone else's.

When we turn our attention within and have the strength to let others make their own mistakes and trust that they will accept help when they are ready, then we have the time and energy to heal ourselves. This of course allows us to come from a place of fullness rather than depletion in our own work. It also gives those around us permission to do the same. It takes a lot of personal power to let go of the part of the ego that needs us to be constantly fixing others in order to feel useful, but I think that it ultimately gives others an opportunity to develop their own personal power.

When you use your power, you will get noticed. Some people will like this and be attracted to you, and some will find it annoying. A lot of the time, the people who have something in themselves that limits their own power, will have the hardest time with yours. You can then heal yourself by realizing that you are not here to please them and that it may have more to do with them than you. Or you may decide to take them on as a project. It is, of course, up to you.

Recognizing and using your healing energy is an incredible experience. Helping someone else can also be amazing. As you do this, your own power will increase; you will be able to accomplish more and have a greater effect on your own life and the lives of others.

Sometimes, though, what is most profound is less about making things happen and more about letting go and allowing things to happen. I have found that my most powerful experiences of healing have been when either through my own meditations or assistance from someone else, I was able to let go and allow something greater to flow through me.

I might call it the Goddess or the Universe or my own healing energy; it probably doesn't matter what I call it. It is the energy and power that is important. When this happens, the experience is much like clearing out mud and sand from a spot in the earth that seems incredibly solid, only to realize that there has been a healing spring waiting to rise up and fill the space created with clear bright water.

SECTION FOUR
ILLUMINATING EXPERIENCES

The Promise

Dream on sweet dreamer... dream
cast your shadows in the sail, and ride the wind
lay your body down before the great bright light
escape the bondage of your body, let go
you shall perceive the night

Live on, dear dove, remember past existences here
becoming one with knowledge you have always known
reaping fruit of seeds you've sown
ten thousand miles beyond the embryonic stage you've grown

And it shall be so, long time to wait, no time to turn your back
It will be known, there is a call, nothing to hold you back... now

Once you sat upon a star, you shone
glory light issued forth from its source
you were the eastern dawn
with iridescent glow your movements catalyzed the energy
you were one with that which makes creation sing
rejoice

Sing on now, sparrow, you shall transcend the wheel
by living out the lives assigned your soul
rejoining that at last which made you whole
so that they might know
there are many things that you will have to learn again
be it so

Beginning at a point in time
you start at once the upward climb
retracing pathways lost forever
multiplying hope, wherever

And it won't be easy
But we'll guide your steps as well as we can
realizing we love you
even though you won't recall who we actually are
... for a moment

Still, it must be your own choice
you will sing, but with your own voice
the message revolves 'round your word
don't try now to comprehend, it will seem too absurd
... until the end
when the ocean ceases pounding the shore
when you finally ask, and receive even more
when the hand brings the rose and your spirits will soar

I woke to the sound of laughter
singing higher pitches than I'd ever heard before
I perceived the beings, pure thought only,
with no physical structure to restrict the flow
they were blue and graceful
dancing gently across vast sandless seas

—Erika Ginnis 1976

CHAPTER 26

Walking on Fire

I have walked on fire a handful of times—seven, maybe eight times in all. It is something that I remember hearing about when I was a child. I saw something in *National Geographic* about indigenous people walking on hot coals. I was fascinated. I don't remember if I pictured myself doing it or not, but watching it even at a young age, I knew it was something significant, something *real*.

To date, I have had two firewalking experiences that have been the most profound: the first time I walked, in June 1996, and a recent walk, in June 2005. This is not to say that the other ones were run-of-the-mill; every time I have had the privilege to walk on fire without being burned, it has been a life-altering experience. However, these two experiences are the ones I am going to share.

Transformation comes in many forms. One is the transformation of self through experience and learning, through uncovering and shedding outmoded thoughts, ideas and beliefs. It is mirrored in the cycle of sprouting, growing, blooming, dying and rebirth present through all of nature, in the seasons, the wheel of the year, as the earth passes through its orbit around the sun.

We (in the Northern Hemisphere) experience Summer Solstice (or Midsummer) near the end of June. Midsummer is the part of the year that is warm and has the most light. This is something that we can physically feel and see, especially here in the Northwest where our days are so much longer and it is still light at 9:30 pm. Midsummer is a visible manifestation of the changes all around us. It is the cycle at its pinnacle, a time of recognition and culmination. We have celebrated and reveled in the summer and warmth, enjoying the glory of nature. As her children, many of us gathered together as a magical family and strengthened our web of support.

Summer Solstice rituals have been some of my favorite rituals for a long time. In fact, when I first thought of pagan ritual, when I was a teenager and hadn't actually attended any, I always brought to mind the summer and the woods. Scenes from *A Midsummer Night's Dream* always drew me in, with the fey and all the mysteries that were brought forth on unknowing mortals.

For me, there has always been a special kind of power in the air around us at the Summer Solstice. It is a time we can not only use the power of the increased light to see far into the evening, but also to illuminate that which is within us that may have been hidden in the darker parts of our own year.

When I first heard that my grove's Summer Solstice ritual would revolve around the activity of firewalking, I wasn't particularly thrilled. You see, I am a water sign; I would have been happier having it involve swimming, and perhaps lying in the sun. The thought of actually building a huge fire for the express purpose of creating a bed of red-hot coals, and then, rather than barbecuing on them, walking across them barefoot, seemed like a really bad idea to me.

It's interesting, in a way, because we all have things that are our boundaries. I have done things in my life of which I had been afraid. I've given psychic readings at fairs where the number of people created an atmosphere which seemed more like the energy of a freeway than anything else. I have experienced the inner knowing of peace and vision in the midst of intense physical sensation/pain. I've jumped off bridges into water a long way down. At one point in my life, I left financial security to "follow my bliss." I have even held fire in my hands. But to walk across it? That was my line, thank you very much.

As the ritual grew closer, I found myself thinking a lot about it and meditating on it, but I hadn't said anything to anyone else. Finally, a few days before the ritual my partner asked me if I was going to walk or not. I told him that I was in some fear around it all, that I wanted to walk but didn't know if I would. I said essentially the same thing to my friend and high priestess when she asked me a day or so later. She seemed to think that this was just the place to be.

I wasn't so sure. It did help to know that she had done quite a bit of firewalking, as had some of my other friends. But regardless of what she or anyone else had done, when it was my turn it would be just me and my precious feet standing before the fire. I decided that it was important that I acknowledge my fear, and also acknowledge my desire. I figured that was about all I could do until the actual event.

I waited for the upcoming day with excitement and concern. I was concerned that I wouldn't be able to tell if it was time for me to walk or not. I had heard people speak of "knowing that now is the time," and I'd been told that I would only know that day at that time if it was right. I was as much afraid of not being certain as I was afraid of being burned. This is an insight that has not been lost on me since.

I came to the ritual in a kind of awe. The setting was so beautiful I felt truly blessed. It was out far from the city, up a long hill. The view was particularly breathtaking. I felt still inside even through the midst of my fear. I felt very held by nature in this place. Our opening ritual had us all name and speak our fears; it was very powerful, and I sensed us come together as a group, young and old. We feasted and built this huge fire, circled around it and energized ourselves, were instructed in the coming firewalk. Then we ate a bit more, danced and allowed the dusk to come along with the coals.

It was time. Part of our instructions was to approach the fire three times, and if we felt the call of the fire only then to walk across. I have since heard that there are many ways to walk fire, but this was the one I experienced, so I listened to this instruction intently. The coals were raked out, so hot that it was uncomfortable to even walk close to them. We were silent, and the energy was building. I knew only one thing for certain, that I wasn't going to be the first person to walk across if I walked at all. But all through the experience, I had this gnawing sense that I would end up walking.

Then the first person walked across. I was amazed. And then another went; I was in wonder. Then I felt the fire call me. Now, as energy workers or pagans, we work with the elements, and fire is certainly one of them. So it seems it shouldn't have been a surprise that fire would have a voice. But it *was* a surprise, and what was even more intense was that it called me by name. The following is what I wrote in my journal the day after the firewalk:

"It was amazing, the actual experience of approaching the fire three times, and hearing it call me by name, to walk through, the feeling of energy and fear rising up and flowing through me. I moved it with my hands up and out the top of my head, felt a call like the draw of a lover—to come, to come, to walk through the fire. And I did it! It reminded me of jumping off a diving board, of dying, that moment when you say 'Oh this is it, it's that time'... that kind of feeling.

"I walked onto the bed of hot coals and walked across it. I didn't feel any heat at all! It was soft as I walked, and that was all. I did it two other times, three times for the Goddess. The only time I felt heat was at the end of the last time at the end of the last run. I felt some hotness on my feet and then I was through. I knew I was done.

"While I was walking I felt totally present... I could shift my attention and one direction would make it start to get warm, the other would cease all temperature. It was so amazing. After I had walked the first time, after I was done. I was so profoundly moved. There were tears in my eyes, thankfulness in my heart. I did it. I did it alone, just me and the fire, and though not alone, me as part of everything, as part of a group, group consciousness that was held in possibility! Yes.

"It was like a baptism! A baptism with fire. This experience went into my subconscious mind... made things real that had only been theories, made things collapse that were lies. Made everything questionable! What is the nature of the universe? If this idea, my idea that fire has to equal burn, if this which was so primal a basis for my reality was false, then what else is actually possible?"

It was walking the talk in a big way.

I was very moved by my experience and by the experiences of all of us there. We really were a group acting for that period of time as a community with a common vision, a vision of successfully and safely walking. The power of the group was palpable, and in fact everyone who attended the ritual walked the fire beautifully and without incident. And I brought away from this solstice a sense of knowing, of how it really feels in the face of the seemingly impossible. I knew beyond a shadow of a doubt, from somewhere deep inside of me, that I would not be burned. I felt it as surely as if I had been walking across a soft mown lawn. I now know what that feels like; I can call it up. I also knew when my time was through and that if I had walked again, without the permission and invitation of the fire, I would surely have been burned.

Transformation is all around us and within us, and we use ritual to pique it or stimulate it or acknowledge it. It takes many forms. At Summer Solstice in that year, it came in the form of walking on fire.

I have the great fortune of being in a group of people (the Sylvan Grove) who honor the earth and her cycles. Since that first firewalk, we have had a tradition of doing it nearly every summer. I have missed some but attended most of them. I have honestly never looked forward to them but have always returned renewed.

In 2005, though, it felt like I was back at the beginning. I had come through a lot of personal changes, and I felt more present than I ever had when it came time for the firewalk. I remember being as afraid as my first time. I tried everything I could think of to avoid going. I was teaching a workshop and couldn't make it (they would wait). I didn't know if my partner wanted to go (he did). I had a friend who was going for the first time, and she was following us to the place outside of town where it was being held (which meant when I saw heavy traffic I couldn't just go home like I wanted to). I have to really love myself and hold in amusement all that I do to avoid change sometimes. I share these things with you now, so that you don't get the idea that you eventually reach some kind of pinnacle of "enlightenment" and never have issues come up!

Once at the site, after the feasting and letting the fire burn down to (really hot) coals, I stood next to the fire and thought to myself, "Hey! That is *fire!* What the heck am I doing here? There is no way I could ever walk on that, *no way* I could have ever walked on that in the past... how did I *do* that before? It just isn't *possible!*" These thoughts were high-pitched and very stressed. I had been convinced that I was not going to walk, and I was wrong.

This time, I felt as raw as the original time I walked, but I was way more conscious of the impossibility of my actions. And therefore, when I did actually walk and for the second time in my life there was *absolutely no heat* once I stepped onto the coals, it changed me profoundly. This time, when the voice called to me it didn't just say my name, it asked, "Do you trust me?" Since the answer, for me, ultimately, was yes, I had to let it all go and walk once more through my fear and into the fire and on to the other side. What a perfect analogy for life.

CHAPTER 27

An Astral Experience

I would like to share with you an experience I had in July 2001. You may see it as a dream or vision, or you may call it an astral experience, as I do. It was an amazing and powerful experience that changed me internally in ways that are difficult to name. I would have, most likely, written about it eventually and actually meant to, procrastinating Pisces that I am; then the events of September 11, 2001, took place, which gave my "dream" even more meaning to me and prompted me to put all this in print. I have found it very helpful over the last few years, given all the turmoil and loss and confusion we have all experienced.

I have kept a dream journal on and off for many years. One of the benefits of having a journal is that you can go back to it and look over what you have written, see the results of the magic you have worked and recall the dreams you have had, which sometimes only make sense months or years later. I hadn't used mine much for a few months. However, that specific July I was teaching my "Inner Journey" class. Whenever I teach a class, I do whatever homework I ask of my students. Since this class uses a dream journal and works with expanding the experience of dreams and astral journeys, I had dusted off my journal and put it on my bedside table.

I am quite a night owl. I went to bed late at night July 10, which was actually early morning July 11, sometime after midnight anyway. I had been reading before bed and had come across a great passage in a book, *The Further Education of Oversoul Seven*, by Jane Roberts, which resonated with me quite strongly even though I had reread the book many times. At the end of a chapter about the birth into a new life of one of the characters, a section talked about the perspective of the Universe opening its eyes for the first time again in each newborn's eyes. I was so struck by this, I put the book down and just let that run through me. I had my focus on the Universe and the amazing divinity ever-present as I went to sleep.

I make a lot of comments about "One-ness" in the notes that follow, since that was the most amazing thing that I experienced. There was no conflict between the One-ness and my experience of the specific energies of the gods and goddesses. The One-ness included All without diminishing any of it. That was part of the point in a lot of ways. No conflict was present even in "seeming" paradox.

I include the notes from my journal just as I made them. I have two main entries about this experience. I will share the first one, then comment, then share the second.

It feels important to let the words that came to me then reach print as I wrote them. I have gone back and forth on how much to paraphrase what I experienced, since there is a lot of repetition (dream journals can be like that); this is my compromise.

When I add a word or two for clarity, I will put it in <brackets>. My journal entries will be shown in italics.

Astral Experience July 11, 2001, Early Morning

The thing I brought back with me was simple, that conflict only occurs as you get down to the slower/lower levels of vibration.

I was experiencing One-ness and God-ness and Higher Self-ness. Hanging out/expanding understanding at energy levels that are way past the physical. In my experience/dream, it all made sense. In that place, I was aware that I had all the information that I needed. It was ALL just fine. There was no conflict, since it was all One thing. There was no conflict among religions, because they were all really one thing.

As I descended back down toward my body, I came back through more and more dense energy. Even still, I could keep a lot of the information intact, and I could put into words the "nonconflict" feel. Then I got to the place the point at which energy splits into poles/dichotomy: male/female, yin/yang. I saw/knew that there was no conflict above this <point> *and that conflict didn't exist at the high levels* <of vibration>. *I also knew that once I came back to the place of "two" (duality) that conflict was then possible again because things had split into two again.*

I still have the memory of, right before I came back to that place, wanting to keep the information and also knowing that to come back to my body I had to re-enter the realm of opposites. I can remember re-entering that realm and descending further and then being above my body and then coming back into my body.

The experience was a visceral experience of God as ONE THING. That we are all already part of or we are one with <God or the Universe; that> *we are already that which is at that high vibration and that we drop below the awareness of this when we descend down into physical reality.*

The feeling of being in the One-ness is hard to describe. One thing that stays with me was this amazing feeling of peace, a sense of being beyond comfort, because there was absolutely no need to be comforted. Everything was all One, all complete and all whole; everything fit perfectly.

One thing that struck me was the very definite delineation between the energy where I experienced everything as all One and the line after which things literally split into two. It reminded me of the horizon line that you see when you are flying in an airplane. It also reminded me of quantum physics, something about splitting a photon of light and getting two electrons that each spin oppositely but are related; you can learn about one particle by measuring the other, even when they are separated by distance. This effect is called nonlocality; Albert Einstein called it "spooky action at a distance."

It was clear this place of nondichotomy was a function of how rapidly the energy was vibrating. Dichotomies came into being when the energy wasn't spinning or vibrating as fast. As it slowed, it became slightly denser and differentiated. Above that point, there was only One. Everything below that point was more than one.

After my experience, I continued feeling the One-ness. I had the feeling that I would always feel this way and that there was no reason to write more about it. But when I went to my chiropractor a couple days later, I told him of my experience, and he said to me, "You have been given a wonderful gift. Write down on paper everything you can remember about it, in as much detail as you can!"

I thought about what he had said and realized that everyday life was drawing me back into its embrace and that if I wanted to remember the lessons from this experience, I needed to do so. Those notes follow.

Notes July 13 and July 14, 2001

The energy was very high—I don't remember going there or getting there, more like I woke up there. I did go to sleep that night with a real "aha" from a book I read, which had the perspective of the Universe opening its eyes for the first time again in each newborn's eyes. I was really in that place of "getting" God-ness when I fell asleep. This I am sure is what propelled me since I had my attention on God/The Universe/The all that IS clearly when I went to sleep.

I remember being in this state. I was conscious—I didn't lose myself, but at the same time I was aware and had the experience that IT was ALL ONE THING—words don't do it justice. I had the visceral experience (even without my body) of this amazing, incredible ONENESS and the complete knowing beyond any doubt that EVERYTHING was totally fine! Completely fine. There was this complete lack of conflict, and I knew that conflict didn't exist here—everything was completely fine and good. There was no contention or discord because it was ALL ONE THING!!

All religions, all ways of being were all fine, there were no problems—there was no this and the other. I was not separate. I was a part of it all, yet still self-aware, and that was all EXACTLY fine. I had all the information I needed—I knew it was all okay and would always be okay

The energy was all one; there was not "other" at this level, and I knew this was very "high" up. The energy was like strata of clouds or bands of energy stacked on one another. I don't know if I had been higher up and came down through that to the point where I knew myself to exist or if I just popped into that state.

It was beyond comforting because there was no discord to be comforted from. It was all incredibly clear, everything, every single thing that exists or once existed was right and included. God was One. Words don't work at all to describe this!

So I know that I had to come back down through all the levels of energy, and I kept a hold of the information that there is no conflict at the higher levels because... THERE IS NOTHING TO BE IN CONFLICT WITH, BECAUSE THERE IS NO "OTHER!"

As I came down through the layers of vibration/energy, I was aware of each of them, and there was this very distinct line that delineated where things split into "two" or "dichotomies." There were a lot of strata between the original place I mentioned and that line. All were slower/lower planes <or> *levels/strata but still existing in the One-ness vibration. Then I was aware of that "line," below which was "two." I knew my physical body was below that line, and so I would need to cross it. I was busy remembering the information from that Highest One-ness experience. I was very conscious of my intention to bring as much of this information back to my body as I was able.*

I knew that a lot was simply not going to translate. For some reason, the piece that stuck with me was the part about conflict and that it didn't exist at "One-ness" at all. It was not possible for it to exist.

It was kind of like an elevator ride. I kept descending into lower/denser vibrations, then passed through that line and there was then "two," the realm of opposites where things split into pairs and such, yin/yang etc. This took place quite a bit higher than where physical reality existed. There was still a number of layers of energy/planes etc. that were between the lines of <that> *delineation and physical reality—so it was still* <all> *at a much higher vibration, even though it was in the separating section.*

I passed down lower and lower and descended still further and kept my consciousness aware of my journey as much as possible. Then I was aware of being above my body and then coming back into my body and waking up—the experience was SO profound I just lay there and thought about it. It was with me all day, and I finally thought I should make some notes about it. I didn't right away (I waited a few hours) because it had really become part of me, down to my cells, and it changed me. It was a totally new perspective. It reminded me of having died and then come back. I was not afraid. I had this real sense of how everything was really all right, completely all right. It was with me like a cloak.

I did write stuff down an hour or so later. I wrote a little more last night <July 13, 2001> *and I did this tonight* <July 14, 2001>. *The effect has lessened, but the knowledge is still present. It was this amazing totally clear memory of knowing that conflict only happens here and that at the higher/*<faster vibratory> *level it just can't, since there is only One thing.*

All religions and ways of being spirit are all just fine. There is no absolutely NO conflict about any of it! None! And that higher level is all one thing. They are ALL right, every single one of them; there is no dissonance at all.

I can still tap into the feeling and memory. Previous to this experience, I figured I understood the idea of One-ness, since I have been meditating for over 20 years. But this was something far beyond what I had previously experienced. It is funny, because I am saying the same words, but now they have a very different grounding. It was such a blessing.

The Internet being what it is, I sent this off to a friend of mine whom I have never met in body but with whom I correspond via e-mail, a fabulous man whose name is Shail Gulhati. He lives in India and started writing to me after reading my article on divination on the Web. He is the author of *The Yogi and the Snake* and *NAAM ROOP*. I had to laugh when I got back his response. He not only understood my experience, but he lives in a culture that has names for it all!

He gave me his permission to include what he wrote in response to my experience.

"My dear Erika, felicitations for your remarkable experience! So, now, you have tasted the sky! The sky is the same; we name it differently.

"All esoteric systems have recorded this marvelous state of One-ness. In Shaivic parlance, the entire manifestation is known to be of 36 evolutes of the cosmic spirit. The top five are steeped with the pristine essence and have no forgetfulness of the divine nature of Self. The sixth evolute is Maya (editor's note: the world and its illusions) and its corollaries, and at this stage the creative divinity veils itself in time, space, efficaciousness, bliss, knowledge, so it does not feel eternal, omnipresent, omnipotent, omniblissed or omniscient.... this "it" is us humans in bodies!

"This is all a veil, though, and we are reduced to duality and think we have a host of limitations. Actually, the design is to rediscover our divinity along with its bliss, and this constitutes the play of manifestation. When we begin to meditate and involute to our original nature, we ascend through the very same stages that we descended! The different stages are marked by astonishment at what really is. "Vismayo yogabhumika," the stations of realization, hold the yogi awed.

"There is a time when we actually cross Maya, and in that state of non-duality we are one. Here, there are not even any thoughts, it is be still and know! This leads to the transformation you have had, never to go away again... you do not have to make an effort to 'keep' it. It has been rediscovered and will remain that way from now on. So felicitations to you. But the sojourn is not over; it has begun! If you remember, in *The Yogi and the Snake*, Shiva says, "Life does not end with enlightenment, it rather has just begun."

The day I woke after my spiritual experience, I remember wondering why it seemed so important to bring back the information about Oneness and non-conflict. What finally got me to write all this down more formally was the events of September 11. I have a feeling now why the information was so pronounced. I will conclude with my final journal entry on this event.

When I wrote the date when all this happened, I noticed it was July 11, 2001. Last Tuesday was exactly two months ago to the day that I had the experience. Last Tuesday's date was September 11, 2001, as we will always remember. I wanted to get this information out finally. I knew it needed to be shared, but I didn't know why until this week. I hope that it does some good and gives some comfort.

CHAPTER 28

An Open Letter from Spirit

This letter came to me in a meditation November 3, 2004. I was looking at world events, and I was disheartened by some things that I thought should be different and yet didn't feel I had any way to change. As is often the case in such situations, I turned to prayer and meditation to shift my perspective and show me a larger view than the one I was seeing.

What I received was very powerful for me and helped me so much that I decided to include it on my Web page and share it with clients. One of the things I have learned over the years is this: If you ask Spirit for guidance and take the time to listen, you will always get an answer. It may not come in the way you expect or say the things you expect to hear, but quite often it is much more lovely.

Of the many things I have included on my Web page, this piece is one of two commented on most frequently. Since people have taken the time to write to me or call to say that is has been helpful to them, I wanted to include it here. I give it to you in exactly the form it came to me, punctuation and all. Take into account that it says some things that address the things in my own life that brought me to that meditation, and if you look closely it even mentions the book you are reading now. Given this, it may at first glance seem person-specific. It's not. Don't be fooled by the appearance. What I know to be true is this: If you are reading it, it is as much for you as it has been for me. It is truly an open letter from Spirit.

"You are the beloved. You are blessed and you are a blessing. I love you and I assure you that you will have everything you need as you need it. Have faith that the way of the world can never outsmart the way of the Most High. You have been given great tools and abilities, do not shun them but rather bring them out into the light and make the way clear for those who will come after you.

"I know that you are saddened by the recent turn of events but let it be for now and it will become clear what this is all about and why this is the way it is, trust me, trust in god trust in the divine expression of love on this planet and know that it is larger than anything that you could ever imagine. Seriously I know that your mind is racing and that you are afraid for the stuff with your money and with the election and with the sadness that you see all around you, but do know please that I am with you and that you are never alone, even now I am here and I am with you and there are many that are with you in spirit.

"And that you can be in the world and not of it and let these things of the flesh pass you by even as you enjoy them, you know that they are not the things that will remain. Remember the light and all that comes out of the light. These are the things that will last. You have great support, draw on it, let it come to use, do not delay the time is now, express your gifts, teach other to express their gifts as well, this is what is needed now. You may think otherwise but the time is upon

you and great changes are afoot. Do not worry about rent, it will be paid, you will be taken care of, do not worry it, let it go.

"Do what you can on your business, create a space for change and growth and for people to reach deep inside themselves, and remember that there are those that are deep in the place that you would call darkness and they are searching for a light, give them something to reach for so that they are not tempted by false things and by promises that have no substance. You can always ask me and I will always answer, I am as close as your very breath.

"Finish your book and get it out there this year, so that others can find it, just finish it don't worry about the publishing that will come, just get it done and start on your next one, you don't have to say everything in this one book, you just need to get the ball rolling so that the light which is you can shine.

"You keep waiting for something to happen for some kind of sign for some kind of something but it has already taken place and you are already at the door and you are already walking through it do not despair it is all right and everything is going to be OK, remember the dream that you had and how everything was all One and that there is no other?

"Well that is real and you know it and you can remember it, feel that, feel that power in the oneness it is true right now right as you sit there typing, thinking that it is your own mind putting the words on paper when you also know that it is not and that I am speaking with you because you are the beloved with whom I am well pleased, really and truly do not despair, let it be.

"I will show you over the next few days, signs to watch for and you will see things and see that I am not gone but I am right next to you and verily right inside of you. Give yourself a chance to be at peace, be kind to your friend he is coming out of utter darkness and he is being challenged at the door and it is hard for him, be kind if you can be. It can only help.

"I am going to let you go now and say to go meditate and meditate on Love and know that you do not have to wait to thrive, you do not have to wait to be happy you don't have to wait to be loved and blessed and abundant, and in fact if you shift how you see things you will see how you are amazingly blessed and loved right at this very moment. Meditate on love and allow yourself to have it wash over you. You are not alone, you have never been alone and this is all only the beginning of great good, mark my words. It is so and it will truly be so. And so it is. I love you.

"P.S. I heard you singing and it was good, thank you for seeking me, I will always answer when you call to me, how could I not, my love for you is beyond measure and without end, really really really. God." ☙

I will leave you with an epilogue, written from my current perspective circa October 2009.

The book took some time, but is now (joyfully) in print. The election that was in question, has come and gone, and our next election surpassed what I could have even conceived of at the time. The rent was indeed paid and has continued to be (in wild and wondrous ways) since this letter was originally "written". My business has grown, I felt called to move from the Pacific Northwest to Hawaii (a lifelong dream), and I am still singing. More things have been revealed since the writing of this book but those things will have to wait for my next installment, until then, all my love, blessed be... and so it is.

About the Author

Erika Ginnis originally from the Pacific Northwest, now lives on the Big Island of Hawaii with her husband Sam and their two cats China and Simba. She has served as a Clairvoyant Reader, Energetic Healer, Ordained Minister, Spiritual Teacher and Writer since 1982. Combining additional study in New Thought, Theta Healing, Astrology, and Ritual Work as a 3rd degree High Priestess in the Sylvan Tradition, she created a private practice called *Inspiration is the Inbreath of Spirit*, that draws from a variety of energetic and healing traditions, and is open to all, regardless of gender, sexual orientation, or religious affiliation.

She offers lectures, workshops and classes in Meditation, Energetic Healing, Inner Journey work, Spiritual Leadership, and Personal Transformation as well as private Spiritual Counseling and Coaching, Healing and Readings. She has had numerous articles published in print and on the web. Including; *The Inner Voice* (*CDM Publications*), *The Goddess Quarterly*, *Kajama*, and *Wiccanweb*. She was a contributing writer and also served on the editorial board of *Widdershins* (*The Northwest Pagan's Choice*) for many years. She is available for sessions in person and over the phone. She can be contacted through her web page. http://www.inbreath.com

LaVergne, TN USA
14 December 2010
208723LV00002B/14/P

9 780982 53660